HISTORIC SCOTLAND

ROMAN SCOTLAND

For Simon and Christopher

HISTORIC SCOTLAND

ROMAN SCOTLAND
Frontier Country

DAVID J. BREEZE

B. T. Batsford Ltd / Historic Scotland

First published 1996

Typeset by Bernard Cavender Design & Greenwood Graphics Publishing
and printed in Great Britain by The Bath Press, Bath

Published by B. T. Batsford Ltd
4 Fitzhardinge Street, London W1H 0AH

A CIP catalogue record for this book is available from
the British Library

ISBN 0 7134 7890 X   (limp)
0 7134 7889 6   (cased)

Front cover
The distance slab found at Hutcheson Hill on the Antonine Wall
(© Hunterian Museum, University of Glasgow).

Back cover
Coin of the Emperor Antoninus Pius issued in 144 to mark the
successful reconquest of southern Scotland
(© Hunterian Museum, University of Glasgow).

Contents

List of illustrations   6
List of colour plates   8
List of tables   8
Foreword by G. S. Maxwell, President of the Society of
Antiquaries of Scotland   9
Preface and acknowledgements   10
Introduction: monuments of our past   11

1   Setting the scene: the sources   13

2   Invasion   30

3   Conquest   53

4   Occupation   70

5   Withdrawal   91

6   External relations   103

Monuments and museums to visit   119
Further reading   121
Index   123

Illustrations

1 The fort at Ardoch 14
2 Roy's map of the Antonine Wall 15
3 Coin of Antoninus Pius 17
4 Coin of Septimius Severus 18
5 Trajan's Column: legionaries cutting down trees 19
6 Ptolemy's map of Britain 21
7 Inscription of 139 from Corbridge 23
8 Inscription from Castlecary 23
9 A writing tablet from Vindolanda 24
10 Excavations at Ardoch in 1897/8 25
11 Brooches from Edinburgh Castle 27
12 Labour camps at Inchtuthil 28
13 Sculpture of legionaries from Croy Hill 28
14 The boar emblem of *legio XX Valeria Victrix* 31
15 The Bridgeness distance-slab 32
16 Coin of Vespasian 33
17 Coin of Domitian 36
18 Ptolemy's map of Scotland 37
19 Trajan's Column: legionaries on the march 39
20 The Dowalton *patera* 40
21 Water flask from Newstead 40
22 Carts on Trajan's Column 41
23 Trajan's Column: a legionary cutting corn 41
24 The camps at Pennymuir 42
25 A tent peg and mallet from Newstead 43
26 A turf cutter from Newstead 43
27 Camps on Trajan's Column 44
28 Tribes according to Ptolemy 44
29 Map of Agricolan marching-camps 46
30 Trajan's Column: a soldier fighting 48
31 The Bridgeness distance-slab 49
32 *Phalerae* from Newstead 50
33 Arthur's O'on 51
34 A marble head from Hawkshaw 52
35 Trajan's Column: soldiers building a fort 54
36 A building inscription from Bearsden 55
37 Carpenters' tools from Newstead 55
38 Military deployment in late first-century Scotland 56
39 Plan of Inchtuthil 58
40 Map of the Gask Ridge 59
41 Artist's impression of a tower on the Gask Ridge 60
42 Hadrian's Wall at Cuddy's Crag 61
43 Map of Hadrian's Wall 62
44 The central sector of Hadrian's Wall 63
45 Map of the Antonine Wall 64
46 The Antonine Wall at Croy Hill 65
47 Artist's impression of the building of the Antonine Wall 65
48 The Antonine Wall ditch at Watling Lodge 66
49 Artist's impression of the Antonine Wall 68
50 The Hutcheson Hill distance-slab 69
51 The Ingliston milestone 69
52 Plan of Elginhaugh 71
53 A fort gate on Trajan's Column 71
54 Artist's impression of the Bar Hill bath-house 72

55 Artist's impression of Bar Hill fort 72
56 Trajan's Column: officers and standard bearers 73
57 Tombstone of Nectovelius from Mumrills 74
58 Artist's impression of Bar Hill headquarters building 75
59 Inscription mentioning cough medicine 77
60 Stamp for eye ointment 77
61 Querns and cooking pots from Newstead 77
62 Wine jars from Newstead 78
63 Face masks from Newstead 79
64 Burnswark 79
65 Ballista balls and sling bullets from Burnswark 80
66 Trajan's Column: a slinger 80
67 An altar from Cramond 81
68 Statue of Mars from Balmuildy 81
69 Head of Fortuna from Bearsden 81
70 Artist's impression of Barburgh Mill fortlet 82
71 Gaming board from Bearsden 82
72 Ships on Trajan's Column 85
73 A wheel from Newstead 86
74 The fort and civil settlement at Inveresk 87
75 Map of pottery made in Scotland 88

76 An altar from Birrens 89
77 A tombstone from Shirva 89
78 A cremation urn from Newstead 89
79 Artist's impression of a native farm 90
80 Inchtuthil nails 91
81 Military deployment in the late first century 93
82 Coin of 154 95
83 Burning at Bearsden fort 95
84 Face-jar of the Emperor Caracalla 96
85 A third-century inscription from Carpow 96
86 Hanoverian forts in Scotland 98
87 The supply base at South Shields 100
88 Military deployment in the mid-second century 101
89 The States of north Britain about 200 104
90 Statue of Brigantia from Birrens 108
91 North Britain in the third–fourth centuries 109
92 The States of north Britain in the late fourth century 111
93 A glass vessel found at Turriff 112
94 ABCD on a stone from Traprain Law 113
95 Moulds from Traprain Law 113
96 Map of finds in Scotland in the third and fourth centuries 114
97 Picts on the Aberlemno churchyard stone 117

Colour Plates

(*Between pages 64 and 65*)

1 A Caledonian war trumpet
2 Constantine the Great
3 A legionary
4 Two auxiliary soldiers
5 Soutra Roman road
6 Durisdeer fortlet
7 The Antonine Wall at Tentfield Plantation

8 Rough Castle from the air
9 Bearsden bath-house
10 The Bearsden latrine
11 The Falkirk hoard
12 The Helmsdale bowls
13 Traprain Law
14 The Traprain Treasure
15 Edin's Hall broch
16 Ardestie settlement

Tables

1 The Roman occupation of Scotland   29
2 The governorship of Gnaeus Julius Agricola   35
3 Family tree of Constantine the Great   105

Foreword

There are many reasons why it gives me great pleasure to write a foreword to this book. As President of the Society of Antiquaries of Scotland, and one whose professional career has been so deeply committed to the study of the Romans in Scotland, I am delighted that Batsford and Historic Scotland should be publishing this volume on such an auspicious occasion. It is almost exactly one hundred years since the Society commenced its pioneering programme of research excavation on suspected Roman sites in the North. Between 1895 and 1910, under the direction of a band of gifted and dedicated Fellows, examples of Roman military architecture began to be recognized in their Scottish setting, and the resoundingly famous names of sites like Inchtuthil and Newstead, Birrens, Camelon and Ardoch, were entered for the first time in archaeology's roll of honour.

That many other Scottish names have subsequently been added to that roll (whose enlargement still shows no sign of abating) we owe partly to that dynamic example provided by those early workers – Abercromby, Barbour, Christison and Macdonald, to mention but a few. Yet we must not forget the richness of the archaeological resource which their present-day successors have been inspired to explore and interpret. Scotland is almost uniquely fortunate in both the variety and the survival-rate of its Roman monuments. It offers to modern scholars and field-workers countless examples of ancient military installations, whose character and function may better be assessed because their place in the contemporary landscape is still readily recognizable. Significantly, the importance of such a resource lies as much in its ability to enhance our understanding of Roman frontier policy in general, as in the light it casts on our national history.

Such contextual significance is tellingly presented here by David Breeze, whose first-hand experience in Roman matters ranges from the study of military organization and its hierarchy to excavation, preservation and heritage-management. And therein lies another important reason for welcoming the appearance of this book: the opportunity its furnishes its author, who has so richly contributed to specialist research in this field, to draw the threads together in a personal picture of his own. History, after all, does not exist as an abstract entity; it is articulated as a series of opinions, and it is often at its most illuminating when those opinions are based, as here, on rich personal experience rather than solely on received truth.

G.S. Maxwell
President, Society of Antiquaries of Scotland

Preface and acknowledgements

This book, like so many, is a personal exploration of its subject, in this case Roman Scotland, and in particular its monuments. I cannot pretend that my view of Roman Scotland is likely to be any more correct than that of any other writer. It is, of course, influenced by the work of others. Of particular importance are the views of my teachers at Durham thirty years ago, Eric Birley, John Mann and Brian Dobson, of John Gillam, Jock Tait and Charles Daniels at Newcastle, and in Scotland Bill Hanson, Lawrence Keppie, Lesley Macinnes and Gordon Maxwell. To all I am grateful for much stimulating discussion over many years. In considering the sources I remain greatly influenced by Leo Rivet's *Town and Country in Roman Britain* (London 1958).

I am grateful to Gordon Maxwell for his Foreword and to Brian Dobson, Jackie Henrie and Chris Tabraham for reading and commenting on the text.

The author and publishers would like to thank the following for their kind permission to reproduce photographs and illustrations: Cambridge University Committee of Archaeology (**44, 64**), Peter Connolly (**colour plates 3 and 4**), The McManus Art Gallery and Museum, Dundee (**85**), W.S. Hanson (**52**), English Heritage (**7**), The Hunterian Museum, University of Glasgow (**3, 4, 16, 17, 50, 68, 77, 82, table 3, front and back covers**), Dr Ernst Künzl, Römisch-Germanischen Zentralmuseum, Mainz (**colour plates 3 and 4**), Angus Lamb (**5, 19, 22, 23, 27, 30, 35, 53, 56, 66, 72**), Michael J. Moore (**41, 47, 49, 54, 55, 58, 70, colour plate 10**), The Trustees of the National Museums of Scotland (**8, 13–15, 20, 21, 25, 26, 31, 32, 34, 37, 51, 57, 59–63, 65, 67, 73, 76, 78, 80, 90, 93–5, colour plates 1, 11, 12, 14**), Society for the Promotion of Roman Studies (**39**), The Royal Commission on the Ancient and Historical Monuments of Scotland (**1, 10, 12, 24, 33**), Ordnance Survey (**6, 18**), Vivian Swan (**84**), Tyne and Wear Museums Service (**87**), The Vindolanda Trustees (**9**).

Introduction: monuments of our past

This book is part of a series published by Batsford and Historic Scotland focusing on ancient monuments and historic buildings. The Roman monuments of north Britain have long interested travellers and writers as well as archaeologists and historians. This is not surprising as Scotland and the upland parts of northern England – and Wales – contain some of the best-preserved military sites surviving anywhere in the Roman empire.

The aim of this book is to explain these monuments and place them in context. Their context is wide. It includes not just Scotland, and Britain, but the whole Roman empire which stretched for nearly 4000km (2500 miles) east to modern Iraq and 3000km (over 1800 miles) south to the Sahara. This is not empty rhetoric. Britain was an integral part of that empire, remaining Roman long after some other parts had been abandoned. Roman emperors visited Britain, soldiers and administrators from many parts of the Roman world helped to govern the province.

Actions on the northern frontier might be directed by the emperor himself. Several emperors visited Britain. This contact started at the very beginning, for Julius Caesar, not strictly an emperor, but certainly progenitor of the first dynasty of emperors, invaded Britain in 55 and 54 BC. The Emperor Claudius followed suit in AD 43, perhaps in conscious emulation of his more famous forebear, when he joined the army of invasion to enter Colchester. The future emperors Vespasian and Titus both participated in the conquest. Eighty years later the Emperor Hadrian came to Britain during one of his major tours of the empire and ordered the construction of the Wall which still bears his name. In 208 the African-born emperor Septimius Severus came to Britain with his sons Caracalla and Geta to campaign against the Caledonians and died at York on 4 February 211. It was at York, too, in 306 that the Emperor Constantius Chlorus died and his son, known to history as Constantine the Great, was proclaimed Emperor by the army of Britain on 25 July of that year, thus throwing over the elaborate scheme of succession arranged by Diocletian and ensuring another period of civil war. His son, Constans, also came to Britain, probably in response to trouble on the northern frontier.

The governors of Britain, particularly in the first and second centuries, were often members of the emperor's council or were his friends; indeed they might be related to him. They also had wide experience of the empire they helped to govern and of its frontiers. The most famous governor of Britain, Julius Agricola, who was unusual in serving three times in the one province, was a personal friend of the imperial family. Service in Britain by other generals was more clearly based on merit. Perhaps the most striking example to illustrate both the cosmopolitan nature of the Roman empire and the importance of the British frontier within it was Statius Priscus. In the face of the threat of war in Britain in 161, Priscus was summoned from the middle Danube where he was governor, only to be moved on to Cappadocia in Asia Minor to deal with an even more serious situation, the massacre of a legion by the Parthians and the subsequent suicide of the provincial governor. Yet personal contacts were always to play an important part in appointments. The commanding officer of *legio II Augusta* during the Antonine advance in the early 140s was A. Claudius Charax from Pergamum in Asia Minor: it is possible that he was chosen to participate in the emperor's triumph through his personal friendship with the Emperor Antoninus Pius himself. Charax's commanding officer in the 140s was Q. Lollius Urbicus, born in North Africa, the home of several other governors of Britain. Urbicus had previously served on the staff of Sextus Julius Severus, formerly governor of Britain, in Judaea, together with Julius Verus, nephew of Severus and himself a later governor of Britain.

The soldiers also might move about the empire. Soldiers from Lower Germany, Raetia (parts of modern southern Germany and Switzerland), Noricum (Austria) and Italy all served in Scotland, as did a local recruit from the tribe of the Brigantes in northern England. Salmanes, who was buried near Bar Hill, had an eastern name and presumably hailed from that part of the world. Large military forces probably drawn from the continental provincial armies as well as the praetorian guard accompanied both Claudius and Septimius Severus on their campaigns.

Roman religion was cosmopolitan. Represented in Scotland are the gods of the Roman pantheon, German goddesses, and Dolichenus from Asia Minor. A procurator made a dedication at Cramond on the Forth to Apollo Grannus, who had cult centres at Faimingen in Raetia and Aachen, both in modern Germany.

Other contacts came through supply. The troops based on the Antonine Wall used pottery manufactured in Britain and in Gaul. Food may have been grown or raised locally, but it was also imported from further afield, probably including the Continent, whence came some of the wine drunk by the army. Armour and other military equipment were also probably imported from the Continent. Merchants will have furthered this trade – and contact – sailing to the mouth of the Rhine, across the Channel and down the west coast of Gaul.

Scotland 1800 years ago was indeed part of a great empire. It nevertheless was on the frontier of that empire, and the surviving monuments – the surviving vestiges of this once great empire – all military in form, bear witness to the fact that Scotland lay on Rome's north-west frontier. As this book is an attempt to place these monuments into their contexts, the focus here is on military affairs. A treatment of the local people and their monuments can be found in Ian Armit's book in this series *Celtic Scotland*.

While chronology underlies the treatment of the evidence, both literary and archaeological, the main approach to Roman Scotland in this book is thematic. After consideration of the sources, the main themes are invasion, conquest, occupation, withdrawal and external relations. In this way, it is hoped, a rounded view can be given of the Roman contact with north Britain nearly 2000 years ago.

CHAPTER ONE

Setting the scene: the sources

The Roman 'period' in Scotland was actually a series of distinct episodes. These varied in length from a single campaign to the absorption of southern Scotland into the Roman empire for a generation: they extended over three centuries from the first Roman contact in the middle of the first century AD. Throughout this period the nature of the contact was essentially military. Scotland in fact was frontier country, lying beyond Hadrian's Wall, which for most of this period formed the north-west frontier of the Roman empire. The Roman army ranged over the land from Hadrian's Wall at least as far as the Moray Firth, while the navy operated on both the west and east coasts and circumnavigated the island.

Roman monuments

No tangible record survives today in Scotland of the Roman navy, but the army has left a remarkable series of remains. Most are in the form of earthworks rather than stone buildings. Individually, none are perhaps as spectacular to visit as Housesteads on Hadrian's Wall, the reconstructed Roman fort at the Saalburg in Germany or Cappidava in Romania, yet, taken as a group, they are indeed remarkable. The surviving earthworks include examples of nearly every type of Roman military structure, a rare combination. They range in size from signal-stations and watch-towers, through fortlets, forts and annexes, and fortresses, to marching-camps, and include at least two frontiers. Together they form one of the main sources for the study of Roman Scotland.

These monuments are not just important visual reminders of Rome, or indicators of what Roman military installations once looked like, but each is a significant archaeological resource in its own right. Their importance is heightened by the relationships between the individual sites which can be developed through observation, survey and excavation. In short, group value is as important as individual site value, and both have been enhanced by the excavations which have been carried out at many sites over the last 100 years.

At the 'massive' end of the scale are several marching-camps, erected by the army for brief sojourns, perhaps of one, two or three nights, and covering up to 67ha (165 acres). Examples of several different series of camps survive in Scotland as earthworks, many with their defended entrances also visible (see **24**). They appear to include camps used during the campaigns of the governor Julius Agricola in the first century and the Emperors Septimius Severus and Caracalla in the early third. At one site, Ardoch, the relationship between overlapping camps can still be observed on the ground. Within the rest of the empire, visible marching-camps are most rare.

Camps were also used to protect the army while undertaking other activities, normally building. Several labour camps are known along the Antonine Wall, though none is visible; others are known outside individual forts. Beside the legionary fortress at Inchtuthil on the River Tay is a labour camp which, on excavation, has revealed evidence for two phases of use (see **12**).

The legionary fortress at Inchtuthil, occupied in the late first century, at 20ha (50 acres) is larger than many temporary camps. Only parts of the rampart and ditch of this fortress are visible today, but excavations over twenty-five years coupled with analysis of aerial photographs have revealed the most complete plan of a first-century fortress known to date (see **39**). No longer visible above ground is the early third-century base at Carpow on the Tay estuary. However, one of the dedicatory inscriptions of this fortress can be seen in Dundee Museum (see **85**).

Forts were generally built for single regiments of 500 or 1000 men, or similar-sized groups. Scotland is fortunate in containing perhaps the most spectacular visible Roman fort earthworks in the empire, at Ardoch (**1**). Here as many as five ditches survive of the north and east defences. To the north lies an annexe, which itself contains a small camp and which overlaps with the southern defences of a 52.5ha (130 acre) camp, which in turn overlies a 25.5ha (63 acre) camp. At Birrens, near the modern border with England, a second fort also has a surviving upstanding rampart with five ditches to the north, though not as spectacular as those at

1 *The fort at Ardoch, Perthshire, from the air looking south. The white arrows indicate the position of the earlier north rampart of the fort, now submerged within the later fortifications. The black arrows point to the corner of a temporary camp lying within the fort's annexe.*

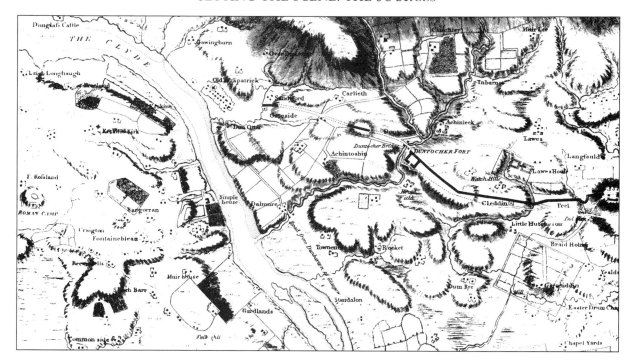

Ardoch. A third well-preserved series of earth-works protects the fort and annexe at Rough Castle on the Antonine Wall (**colour plate 8**).

Several fortlets also survive. These are small outposts built for about eighty soldiers or fewer, and usually only protected by a single rampart and ditch (see **70** and **colour plate 6**). Even smaller were the signal-stations or watch-towers, similarly defended by a rampart and ditch. The most important group of these lies beside the Roman road running along the Gask Ridge in Perthshire and appears to have formed part of an early frontier dating to the late first century (see **41**).

Some fifty years later another frontier – the Antonine Wall – was built across central Scotland (see **46** and **colour plate 8**). Today, substantial lengths of this survive as earth-works. In addition to the rampart and ditch are forts at Rough Castle and Bar Hill, the latter containing the remains of its headquarters building and bath-house – a second bath-house is visible at Bearsden (**colour plate 9**) – a fortlet, several 'expansions' (perhaps beacon-plat-forms) and the connecting road, the Military Way. Long stretches of road exist elsewhere in

2 *Part of William Roy's map of the Antonine Wall surveyed in 1755. This section shows the fort at Duntocher near the western end of the Wall.*

Scotland, some, as at Rough Castle, with quarry pits lying beside them.

Training was an important element in the success of the Roman army. While no parade ground has yet been identified in Scotland, at Burnswark there survives what appears to have been a training area for the army of the north, where exercises could be undertaken at the site of an abandoned Iron Age hill-fort (see **64**). A second training area has been claimed for Woden Law, but this identification is not certain.

Many of these monuments survive in the uplands of Scotland and their preservation has been aided by beneficial land-management regimes, in particular sheep-farming. A list of monuments and museums to visit is provided at the end of the book.

We are fortunate too that our forebears recorded these remains through description and survey. Justly the most famous – and most accurate – of these was William Roy, who went on to found the Ordnance Survey (**2**). His survey of Roman Scotland was undertaken in the aftermath of the 1745 Jacobite Uprising, but was not published until 1793, three years after his death. Systematic survey is now primarily undertaken by the Royal Commission on the Ancient and Historical Monuments of Scotland. Since 1945 survey on the ground has been supplemented by aerial photography (see **12**). This has not only amplified existing knowledge, but has also added wholly new classes of monuments to the portfolio of Roman Scotland, in particular fortlets and small enclosures on the Antonine Wall.

Literary sources

The surviving sites are eloquent testimony to the former presence of the Romans in Scotland. The framework within which these were built and occupied is provided by surviving Roman documents and literary texts. These give a broad outline of events on the northern frontier and particular details of certain occasions, usually when a member of the imperial family was involved. The exception to this was the governorship of Gnaeus Julius Agricola from 77 to 83. He had the good fortune to have as his son-in-law the famous historian Cornelius Tacitus. Tacitus wrote a biography – perhaps hagiography would be a better word – of his father-in-law, which is not just the only significant source of information for the governorship of Agricola, but also the major source of information for the forty years from the invasion of 43.

It is through Tacitus that we know that the first major invasion of Scotland took place about 79 under Agricola and from him we also receive a hint at the date of abandonment of the conquests. Another biography, this time of the Emperor Antoninus Pius, records the occasion of the next invasion of Scotland, but not the date within his reign (138–61). The third major invasion took place under the Emperor Septimius Severus (193–211) in the early third century: this also is recorded in the literary

sources, which date the events to the last years of the emperor's reign. One of the historians who wrote about that invasion was Cassius Dio, a contemporary of Severus and a senior official of the Roman empire whose *History of Rome* is also a useful source for the events of earlier centuries. Each of the three main invasions resulted in the occupation of Lowland Scotland – the Romans, so far as we know, never occupied any part of the Highlands. The last period of occupation was brief, cut short by the death of Severus.

Our sources can be very frustrating, not mentioning when and where events took place, where the enemy lived, nor which Wall was crossed. We are not absolutely sure of the dates of Agricola's governorship, though the earlier date of 77–83 is accepted here. Tacitus is extremely sparing with geographical details, which would have been of little interest to his readers (though Agricola's staff presumably collected information which was passed on to appear in Ptolemy's *Geography* in the mid-second century: see **18**). Tacitus does not state where Agricola's second season of campaigning took place and is similarly silent on the location of the fifth season, beyond the clear implication that it was on the west coast. He does not tell us where the battle of Mons Graupius was fought, apart from the fact that it was beyond the Forth, though he does tell us that it was late in the season, that after the battle Agricola sent a fleet to sail round Britain which apparently visited the Orkney islands, and that the army returned to the province through the territory of fresh nations. It is ironic that we are unable to determine where Mons Graupius took place because Tacitus wrote his account of Agricola's governorship to culminate in this event.

Nevertheless, Tacitus does provide considerable information on the campaigns. Agricola arrived in Britain late in the season and immediately dealt with a rebellion by the Ordovices of central and north Wales who had presumably been subdued by his predecessor, Julius

Frontinus. The year was probably 77. No location is provided for the activities of the following summer, but Tacitus records that in his third season Agricola ravaged as far north as the Tay. The fourth season was spent consolidating the territory gained and a chain of garrisons was placed across the Forth–Clyde isthmus. The fifth season started with a naval expedition and included subduing nations hitherto unknown. During the campaign, Tacitus informs us, Agricola drew up his troops facing Ireland and considered invasion. The sixth and seventh seasons were both spent north of the Forth. In the sixth, Agricola 'fearing a general rising of the northern nations' moved north, but nearly lost the ninth legion in a night attack on its camp. This was redeemed in the final season through victory at Mons Graupius. Agricola soon after returned to Rome at the end of an unusually long governorship.

Agricola's northern conquests were of short duration: Tacitus was to write, 'Britain was conquered and immediately lost'; hyperbole undoubtedly, but nevertheless with sufficient truth presumably not to be laughed out of court. The following decades are dark and it is not until the reign of the Emperor Hadrian that there are helpful references to Britain in the literature. At the beginning of the reign (117), we are told, Britain could not be kept under control – perhaps a reference to the northern frontier – and in 122 Hadrian (117–38) himself came to Britain and ordered the construction of a wall 117km (80 Roman miles) from sea to sea to divide the Romans from the Barbarians.

The next reign, that of Antoninus Pius (138–61), started with another change in policy (3). His biographer tells us that he 'waged many wars, using his legates. Lollius Urbicus, a legate, conquered the Britons for him and when he had driven the barbarians off, built another wall, of turf.' We are not informed, however, where that wall, the Antonine Wall, lay nor when it was abandoned. The biography of Marcus Aurelius (161–80) states that on his

3 *The successful reconquest of southern Scotland was recorded on the coinage of the Emperor Antoninus Pius. This coin was issued in 144 and shows the emperor on one side and Britannia on the reverse.*

accession in 161 'war was also threatening in Britain and the Chatti had invaded Germany and Raetia. Calpurnius Agricola was sent to deal with the Britons and Aufidius Victorinus with the Chatti.' We do not know where in Britain the war threatened and can only assume that it was on the northern frontier.

In describing the reign of the Emperor Commodus (180–92) Cassius Dio records that 'his greatest war was in Britain. The tribes in the island crossed the wall which separated them from the Roman legions, did a great deal of damage, and cut down a general and his troops; so Commodus in alarm sent Ulpius Marcellus against them. Marcellus inflicted a major defeat on the barbarians.' In 197, following the successful culmination of Septimius Severus' bid for the purple, there was again trouble on the northern frontier, recorded for us by Dio. 'The Caledonians instead of honouring their promises had prepared to defend the Maeatae, and Severus at that time was concentrating on the Parthian war; so Lupus [governor of Britain] had no choice but to buy peace from the Maeatae for a considerable sum of money, recovering a few captives.' This passage is particularly interesting in demonstrating the existence of treaties between Rome and her northern neighbours as well as the payment of money to them.

Ten years later, there was warfare again in Britain, only this time the Romans were being successful. Notwithstanding those victories, in

208 the Emperor Septimius Severus decided on a new forward policy in Britain. We are even given the reasons for this change of policy: the emperor wanted to get his sons away from the flesh-pots of Rome 'so that they might come to their senses in the disciplined life of the army'; 'the armies were becoming slack through inactivity'; 'there was a rebellion among the barbarians and they were laying waste the country, plundering and causing widespread destruction'; and Severus 'enjoyed winning renown and after victories and titles he had won in the east and north he wanted to raise trophies over the Britons as well'. It must be said that it is far from clear that there was trouble on the northern frontier sufficiently serious to warrant the presence of the emperor. The same phraseology used for the appeal from the governor of Britain to the emperor, that 'the defence of the place required more troops or the emperor's presence', was used on another occasion elsewhere. Dio informs us that Severus' intentions were the completion of the conquest of the whole island and that he almost reached the end of the island, but otherwise the location of the campaigns is not recorded (4). Dio's – and Tacitus' – accounts of the fighting tactics of the northern tribes are important, as we will see.

Each of these invasions and occupations was at least partly recorded and described in the literary sources, but other events occurred which are less well recorded and therefore less well known and whose implications are scarcely perceived. The invasion of the province of Britain by the northern tribes in about 180 was clearly serious, but we know nothing of the counter-measures which the governor, Ulpius Marcellus, took. Further, there may have been events not recorded in the literary sources. An inscription of 158 from Hadrian's Wall, now unfortunately lost, recorded rebuilding. This should indicate that the Wall was being reoccupied and the Antonine Wall abandoned, but no literary source hints at any such action.

The various withdrawals from Scotland are similarly dark to us. No Roman literary source informs us exactly when Agricola's conquests were abandoned nor when and why the Antonine Wall was abandoned. Dio and Herodian, however, are more informative on the events following Severus' death. We are informed that his son, Caracalla (see **84**), 'made treaties with the enemy, evacuated their territory and abandoned the forts'.

For nearly a whole century after 211 we have little literary or documentary evidence of contact between Rome and the northern tribes. At the end of that century, however, a Roman author first mentions Rome's new enemy in the north, the Picts. It is against the Picts that the Emperor Constantius Chlorus campaigned in 305 and his son, Constantine the Great (**colour plate 2**), some years later, and it was probably the same enemy which brought Constantine's son, Constans, to Britain in the winter of 342/3 (the date is provided by a law promulgated in Boulogne on 25 January 343). None of these invasions appears to have been intended to result in new conquests for the empire: they were merely punitive expeditions. The Picts continued to put the Romans on the defensive right up to the end of the century. In 360, 'the savage tribes of the Scots and Picts were carrying out raids in Britain, having disrupted the agreed peace, and laying waste places near the frontiers'. A force was dispatched from the Continent to restore order. Seven years later 'a conspiracy of the barbarians had brought Britain to her knees', one general had been

4 *Coin of the Emperor Septimius Severus recording his victory in Britain.*

killed, another circumvented. Again a field army was sent from the Continent, which, under its general, Theodosius, 'restored cities and the garrison's fortresses and protected the frontiers with sentries and forts'.

It is important to appreciate that few of the literary sources were written by disinterested people. Tacitus was the son-in-law of Agricola. So far as we know, he did not invent or falsify events but he may have embroidered them, placed Agricola's actions in the best light and perhaps omitted those which did not. Many of his comments are *topoi*, set phrases normally applied to invite comparison with the best generals or the best administrators, while the turning of an apt phrase was more important than boring details about Britain. Tacitus and most Roman authors are frustrating in their lack of information. One yearns for something a little better than continual references to the woods and marshes of Caledonia (5).

The sheer fact that Britain lay on the edge of the known world lent it an air of mystique. This

5 *This scene on Trajan's Column shows legionaries cutting down trees while building a road. Shields and helmets stand in the foreground while the soldiers wield their axes. The wars shown on Trajan's Column were fought between the Agricolan and Antonine invasions of Scotland.*

continued up to the very end of Roman Britain when contemporaries wrote as if the island had been only recently discovered or conquered. It remains difficult, too, to know how exact these writers were in their use of terminology. When even Tacitus can ascribe Boudica to the wrong tribe, how can we be sure that Vettius Bolanus really did reach the Caledonian plain during his governorship, 69–71, as Statius averred? How could the Brigantes invade part of the province, as Pausanius stated, when they were part of it? Are words simply being used for effect, or loosely, rather as 'English' is used today when it ought to be 'British'?

Problems of precision are exacerbated because few of the sources are contemporary

19

with the events they describe. Tacitus obviously had first-hand information from his father-in-law, Agricola, while Dio was not only a contemporary of Septimius Severus but a high-ranking officer in the imperial civil service, being consul twice and a member of the council of Severus and Caracalla. His contemporary, Herodian, however, clearly had little knowledge of imperial affairs. Ammianus Marcellinus was also a contemporary of the events he described in the late fourth century. But other authors were describing actions which had occurred many years, sometimes centuries, earlier. The references to the construction of both Hadrian's Wall and the Antonine Wall, for example, appear in fourth-century biographies of the two emperors. Even the information Ptolemy included in his *Geography* was third-hand.

Contemporary sources suffer from their own problems. Agricola and his son-in-law, Tacitus, were strong supporters of the Flavian dynasty, whose last member, Domitian, was a tyrant, damned after his murder in 96. Tacitus wrote under a new emperor, Trajan, who was as loved by the senatorial nobility as Domitian had been hated. Tacitus accordingly was in a most difficult position, as a Flavian supporter, in writing about those years and one result is likely to have been to play down Domitian's part in policy decisions and enhance Agricola's. To some extent the *Agricola* is a justification of the service of loyal members of the aristocracy, even to a 'bad' emperor.

From the fourth century much information survives in panegyrics: speeches in praise of emperors and high officials. The language can be so flowery that it almost hides the achievements which are being praised and certainly encourages scepticism. The mere fact that Ammianus Marcellinus wrote his *History of Rome* in the reign of the Emperor Theodosius, the son of the general who recovered Britain after the 'Barbarian Conspiracy' of 367, was sufficient to ensure extensive treatment of the exploits of the father.

The literary sources also suffer from another disadvantage: they rarely explain why something happened, and, even when they do, the explanation has to be carefully weighed, as does any explanation of a political action today. We are never informed of Agricola's long-term aim. We can only presume that it was the conquest of the whole island, because that would have been within the framework of contemporary Roman expansionist policy. The reason for the construction of Hadrian's Wall is given by his biographer, to separate the Romans from the barbarians, but not the reason for the move north to the Antonine Wall. Septimius Severus, we are explicitly told by Dio, came to Britain intending to conquer the rest of the island. Our sources do occasionally also furnish the Romans' justification for their actions. Agricola moved north of the Forth in 82 because he feared the threatening movement of the Caledonians. An enigmatic passage in Pausanius' *Description of Greece* states that the Emperor Antoninus Pius deprived the Brigantes of part of their territory because they had attacked the Genounian district. Here, perhaps, is hidden the *casus belli* for the Antonine invasion of 140, but we do not know where Genounia was, while the Brigantes were already part of the empire so should have been firmly under control.

The literary sources provide evidence of history, ethnology and geography. Ptolemy's *Geography*, written in the mid-second century, reveals considerable knowledge of north Britain, including its shape, the name of its capes, rivers and islands, as well as its people, or rather their tribes and settlements (**6**). Strangely, while the information is detailed, the basic map is wrong, for Scotland north of the Tay is turned through 90°. It seems possible that this twist is the result of the Greeks' preconceptions about the world: they believed that life was not possible beyond 63°N. Ptolemy knew, however, that if northern Britain was drawn out as a map it would stretch to 66°N, with Thule beyond, so he

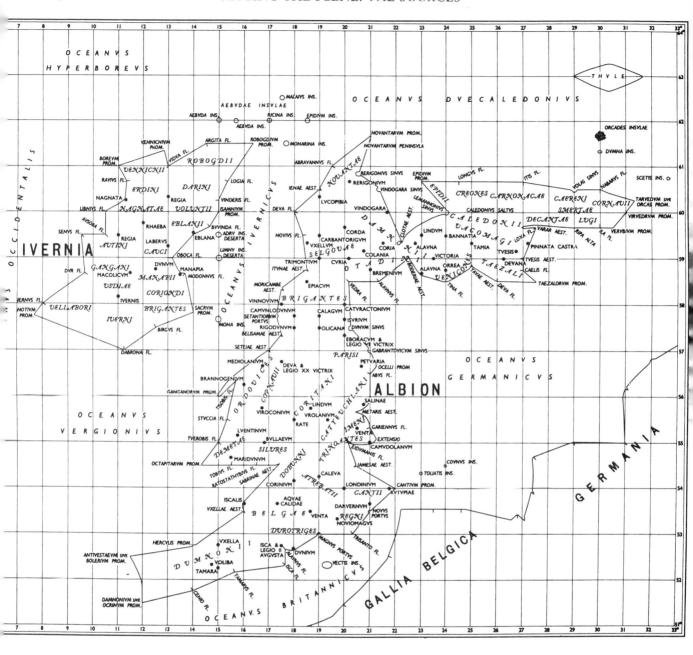

turned the northern part of the island in order to keep it south of that line of latitude. If the fault is rectified, then Scotland looks more or less correct (see **18**).

A further group of literary sources is provided by the military treatises. These include not only two works on the Roman army, Vegetius' *de re militari* and the anonymous *de metatione castrorum*, but also excursions on

6 *Ptolemy's map is not a bad depiction of Scotland, showing the tribes and various place-names. It was the result of over four centuries of collecting geographical knowledge.*

the army in, for example, Polybius' *History of Rome* and Josephus' *Jewish War*. Together with the writings of Caesar, Tacitus and Ammianus Marcellinus these provide incomparable information on the organization and fighting tactics of the army.

The literary sources provide one form of written evidence for events on the northern frontier. They are supplemented by coins, inscriptions and documents.

Coins

Coins can often provide dates for events described by the historians; sometimes the coins even illustrate the actual events themselves. A coin issue of late 142 or 143 provides the date of the successful completion of the Antonine advance which is not specified in the literary sources (see **3**). The victory of the governor Ulpius Marcellus over the northern tribes was celebrated by a special coin issued in late 183–4; again the literary sources do not date the invasion within the emperor's reign. Both these coin issues show Britannia on the reverse.

Septimius Severus issued many coins relating to his British expedition of 208–11. Several in 208 showed Severus and Caracalla riding to war, while one rare coin issue portrayed a galley containing military standards, indicating a sea voyage. A bridge of boats appeared on a coin of 209 while several showed the emperors riding down their foes. Victory was celebrated by another special issue in 210 when the emperors took the title *Britannicus* (see **4**).

Inscriptions

While the literary sources provide a framework for the history of the northern frontier, inscriptions from the forts and from the Antonine Wall furnish additional information. Inscriptions also have an advantage over the literary sources: they generally mean what they say. Scotland is particularly rich in inscriptions, and we are fortunate in that so many have been carefully collected and preserved over several centuries. These include highly ornamented slabs recording the construction of the Antonine Wall, building stones, dedications and tombstones. Inscriptions furnish

evidence relating to the building of forts and frontiers, the regiments based there, the careers of soldiers, the wives of officers and other civilians who accompanied the army.

Most of the inscriptions date from the second-century occupation. A particularly important inscription at Corbridge just south of Hadrian's Wall records the construction of a building by the army in 139 (**7**). This inscription, together with its partner erected in the following year, date the fort rebuilt at this time. Corbridge was intimately linked to Dere Street and occupation further north: rebuilding here suggests that preparations were already in hand for the Antonine advance in 139, within months of Hadrian's death in July 138. Inscriptions from the Antonine Wall not only help us to determine accurately that this frontier was indeed the Antonine Wall but also confirm the involvement of Lollius Urbicus in the construction of one of its forts. An inscription from Puteoli in Italy demonstrates that the Emperor Antoninus Pius had taken the title *imperator*, 'Conqueror', by 142, indicating the successful completion of the conquest of southern Scotland. Literary evidence, coins and inscriptions accordingly combine to demonstrate that the Antonine advance north was planned and executed within the years 139–42.

A single inscription from the legionary base at Carpow on the Tay not only demonstrates its Severan date but suggests that the fortress was not abandoned as precipitately as Dio would have us believe. The inscription appears to date to the sole reign of Caracalla which did not begin until 212 when he murdered his brother, Geta, just a year after the death of their father.

We have already seen that the literary sources are poor at illuminating some events, in particular the abandonment of the Agricolan conquests in the late first century and the Antonine occupation in the mid-second century. Inscriptions are no assistance here as they were erected to commemorate building not destruction or withdrawal. Nevertheless, occasionally an inscription can

7 *This dedication slab records the construction of a building at Corbridge by* legio II Augusta *during the second consulship of the Emperor Antoninus Pius (139) and the governorship of Q. Lollius Urbicus.*

demonstrate that a fort was still occupied at a certain date. Thus an inscription from Castlecary on the Antonine Wall can be shown probably to date to the period 175–90 (8).

To inscriptions on stone we can add the metal diplomas, certificates of privileges, which were issued to soldiers. These are a valuable source of information on historical events, the governors of the province and the strength of the Roman army in Britain, as the diplomas were issued in batches and all the

8 *The erection of a shrine to Mercury is recorded on this altar erected at Castlecary on the Antonine Wall. It was dedicated by soldiers of* legio VI Victrix, *who were citizens of Italy and Noricum. They had probably been transferred from* legio II Italica, *raised in Italy in 165 and thereafter stationed in Noricum. The inscription probably dates to between 175 and 190.*

regiments in each group were listed. A diploma of 17 July 122 mentions both the retiring governor, Pompeius Falco, and his newly arrived successor, Platorius Nepos, who himself appears on the building inscriptions on Hadrian's Wall. The issuing of two diplomas for the British army in 146 may imply a larger than normal discharge, which may be related to the completion of work on the Antonine Wall. A recently discovered diploma of 178 records the presence in Britain of Ulpius Marcellus, the governor, we are informed by Dio, who was sent to deal with the invasion by the northern tribes during the reign of the Emperor Commodus. Commodus was joint emperor with his father, Marcus Aurelius, from 176, but sole emperor from 180 until his murder in 192. While the affirmation that Ulpius Marcellus was governor in 178 confirms the evidence of one inscription, at Benwell, which refers to two emperors, a second inscription (from Chesters) records Marcellus serving under one emperor. Did Marcellus return to Britain to deal with the invasion, or was Dio being flexible in the reference to the beginning of the new reign, starting it in 176 when Commodus ruled jointly with his father rather than 180 when he became sole emperor?

A new and most exciting source for the northern frontier are writing tablets (9). The greatest collection, of international importance, has been found at Vindolanda by Hadrian's Wall, with Carlisle producing a few: some were apparently discovered at Newstead during the 1905–10 excavations, but they can only be recognized with hindsight. The Vindolanda writing tablets are important not just for the light they cast on everyday life on the northern frontier, but in their similarity to military documents found in North Africa, Egypt and Syria. Formerly, it might have been possible to argue that the eastern documents were only relevant to that area, which had a greater history of literacy and civilization. The similarity in style of the documents from both ends of the empire emphasizes that north Britain was a full part of the Roman empire and validates the use of the eastern documents as evidence by analogy.

The writing tablets have come to light during archaeological excavations, the major source of new information, and it is to this work which we must now turn.

Excavation and survey

Modern excavation of Scotland's military remains began 100 years ago. In 1890 the Glasgow Archaeological Society started a series of investigatory excavations along the line of the Antonine Wall which demonstrated that the Wall was indeed of turf construction, as Antoninus Pius' biographer had stated 1500 years before. In 1895 the Society of Antiquaries of Scotland commenced a series of excavations of Roman sites which continued for nearly twenty years. Today the excavations read like a

9 *This writing tablet found at Vindolanda is a list of food. Readable on lines 3–7 are* condimen[torum] *(of spices),* capreum *(goat),* salis *(salt),* porcellum *(young pig),* pernam *(ham); lines 9–10* frumen[ti] *(of corn),* ceruin[am] *(venison).*

roll of battle honours: Birrens 1895, Ardoch 1896–7 (**10**), Burnswark 1898 (see **64**), Camelon 1900, Kaimes Castle and the Gask Ridge 1900, Inchtuthil 1901, Lyne 1901, Castlecary 1902, Rough Castle 1903 (**colour plate** 8), Newstead 1905–10, Cappuck 1911–12. Excavations have continued up to the present day and continue to provide new and significant information about Roman Scotland.

The primary aims of such excavations are to determine the plan of each site at each period of occupation and to trace its history. It is also important to understand the uses of the buildings and how their inhabitants lived within them. A remarkable example of use occurred in 1903 when an inscription found during excavations at Rough Castle proved that the headquarters building was termed the *principia* not the *praetorium* as had hitherto been believed. Modern scientific techniques have extended the range of questions we can ask – and answer. Today, all excavators would acknowledge, for example, that knowledge of the countryside in which a fort was built is important, as is the effect which the Roman army had on that countryside.

Early archaeologists were keen to discover the plans of the structures they excavated. This

10 *Excavations in progress at Ardoch in 1897/8. Revealed are remains of one of the few stone buildings.*

was relatively straightforward when the buildings were of stone, as, for example, at Birrens. Timber buildings offered more of a challenge, but were not totally elusive even 100 years ago as the observation skills of Thomas Ely, the Society of Antiquaries' Clerk of Works at Ardoch, demonstrated. The plans of the timber buildings his workmen uncovered are perfectly recognizable today and open to interpretation.

It was also appreciated that there might be more than a single period at certain sites. At Newstead, for example, James Curle was able to enumerate as many as five phases, assigned to two main periods, Agricolan and Antonine. Two phases were allocated to the first century and, though Curle could not determine the date of the end of this period, he could see that it was some time after 86 but before about 120: indeed he saw Newstead as part of a 'strategic line' held after the 'abandonment of Agricola's forts between the Forth and Clyde'. Reoccupation occurred under Antoninus Pius, was broken briefly in 158, and thereafter continued until the early 180s. Curle's framework has proved vital and still forms the basis of our present chronology of Roman Scotland.

Curle realized that there was no Severan occupation at Newstead: in fact he knew of no Severan site in Scotland. Severan occupation continued to be elusive until the 1960s when an indubitable third-century fort was proved, Carpow on the Tay.

Curle recognized that literary evidence and inscriptions could provide firm start dates for the various periods of occupation but it was an altogether more difficult problem to date the end of each period. For assistance he turned to the archaeological artefacts. Coins are the most useful for they bear their date of manufacture. Unfortunately coins might remain in circulation for years, if not decades, and the age of the coin on loss can only be estimated roughly from the amount of wear it has suffered. The absence of coins can be as instructive as their presence. Recently it has been persuasively argued that the absence of the relatively common coins of 87 from northern forts – in comparison to those of 86 which do occur on Scottish sites – indicates that Agricola's conquests were abandoned in 87 or, at the very latest, early 88, the latest date that the coins of 87 would have appeared at the Scottish forts if they had been occupied. This is the best evidence we have for the date of the withdrawal from Scotland and is striking support for Tacitus' comment that Britain was conquered and immediately abandoned.

Unfortunately coins are not as clear in helping to determine the date of the abandonment of the Antonine conquests. The latest accurately provenanced coin from a second-century fort is of the Empress Lucilla dated to 164–9. It was found in a granary in the fort at Old Kilpatrick, but the excavator did not make clear the precise stratigraphical position of the coin. There are a few later coins from the Antonine Wall, but they are all stray finds and their significance is uncertain.

Pottery too is important in helping to date certain events, but it is less helpful on the northern frontier than elsewhere for it is the northern frontier itself which provides the base lines for dating pottery as the frontier installations are independently dated by literary references and inscriptions. Nevertheless, pottery can be useful when used for comparative purposes within an area or when compared to dated frontiers elsewhere. Thus it has been argued from study of the imported pottery generally called samian ware that the Antonine forts in Scotland were abandoned in about 163. Later samian is found on other sites in Scotland, but only on civilian not military settlements.

Artefacts, however, are not just valuable as dating evidence (11). They help us understand how the soldiers lived in their forts; they provide important information on contacts, between the Romans and the local population, between the army and its suppliers, on religious beliefs, and on the level to which the local people adopted Roman civilization, though this is more difficult to measure. Recent research, for example, has resulted in the appreciation that much more pottery was made in Scotland than previously realized (see 75) and this has significant implications for the whole framework of the supply of the army on the northern frontier.

Excavation is also the only source of information on civilian sites, whether outside Roman forts or in the countryside. We know little about civil settlements outside forts. Roman artefacts, until the discovery of radiocarbon dating, were the only source of dating evidence for native sites and for most sites they remain the only dating material. Unfortunately Roman artefacts might remain in circulation after the army had departed so their presence must be treated with caution.

As we have seen, most new sites today are discovered through aerial reconnaissance (12). When combined with excavation, especially, this provides a powerful tool to help understand the nature of the patterns of invasion and occupation. Roman forts were generally located a day's march apart, perhaps 22km (14

11 *A trumpet brooch and a dragonesque brooch, dating to the late first to mid-second centuries, found during recent excavations at Edinburgh Castle.*

miles). If the distance between two known forts on a particular route is too great, then it is a reasonable assumption that a fort will exist in between. Aerial reconnaissance has been very successful in finding such forts.

Aerial photography has also been particularly successful at discovering marching-camps. The growth in such discoveries since 1945 has allowed the camps to be classified into different series. Excavation thereafter has resulted in the establishment of stratigraphical relations and the assignment of specific series of camps to specific campaigns. This in turn has led to a recognition that the differences in the morphology of camps may be significant. It would appear that first-century camps tend to be square in shape, while later camps are rectangular.

It must be admitted that there is little hard archaeological evidence to date specific camps, which by their very nature were short-lived and therefore unlikely to yield many artefacts, but new evidence has come forward to challenge past assumptions. This evidence takes two forms: structural and artefactual. Recently there has been a number of extensive excavations of camps. These have demonstrated that some sites exhibit more than one phase of activity even though this is not visible on aerial photographs. Other large-scale excavations have produced pottery which has forced reconsideration of the dates of certain camps. No doubt this refining of the data will continue.

Evidence by analogy

Scotland's Roman fort and frontiers were constructed by an army which held sway over one of the greatest empires which the world has seen. Surviving evidence from elsewhere in the empire helps us understand the military monuments of Scotland. The Roman army left records of its activities from the Atlantic Ocean to the Caspian Sea, from the North Sea coast of Germany to the middle of the Sahara Desert. These records include its constructions, sculpture (**13**), artefacts including weapons and armour, military treatises, inscriptions, parchments and papyri. The same army and officer corps operated across the whole empire within the same legal and administrative framework. Thus evidence by analogy is provided for the army of Britain.

27

12 *An aerial photograph of the labour camps outside the legionary fortress at Inchtuthil. Inside the camps, rows of pits are clearly visible.*

13 *This sculpture of three legionaries was found at Croy Hill on the Antonine Wall. It may have been part of a tombstone showing a father and his two sons. Each soldier wears a cloak over his armour and carries a shield, helmet and spear: the figure to the right also holds a drawn sword. This tombstone could have been found anywhere in the Roman empire and emphasizes the value of evidence by analogy.*

The opinions of modern scholars

In an influential essay on sources of evidence, Leo Rivet included the opinions of modern scholars. These, indeed, are very relevant. The way that scholars have interpreted the sources over the last 250 years significantly affects how we view the subject today. It is, in fact, very difficult to escape from the strait-jacket of past thought. Hence it is crucially important always to keep the original evidence in mind when attempting to understand Roman Scotland and its material remains.

Modern research might be said to start in the middle of the eighteenth century with the publication of John Horsley's *Britannia Romana* in 1732 and William Roy's survey of Scotland twenty years later (see **2**). Many of the conclusions reached by these two acute observers remain relevant today and are now overlain by the writings of later archaeologists such as Francis Haverfield, R. G. Collingwood, George Macdonald, Ian Richmond, Eric Birley, Kenneth Steer and Anne Robertson, who have all helped shape our understanding of Roman Scotland.

The literary, epigraphic, numismatic and archaeological evidence, as well as the monuments themselves, allows us to gain an appreciation of the nature and the effect of the presence of the army on both the conquered and unconquered people of Scotland (**table 1**). The tangible expressions of the contact between Scotland and the Roman empire survive today in the earthworks of the installations built by the Roman army and in the artefacts and inscriptions in Scotland's museums.

Table 1 The Roman occupation of Scotland

This table offers a succinct presentation of the evidence for the dates and durations of the various periods of Roman occupation in Scotland.

period	literary sources	inscriptions	coins	pottery
FLAVIAN I (conquest of Lowland Scotland as far as the Highland Line) starts 79 ends 87/88	Tacitus		coins of 86 no coins of 87	
FLAVIAN II (some forts held in southern Scotland) starts 87/88 ends *c*. 103–5			coin of 103	
ANTONINE I (reconquest of southern Scotland as far north as the Tay) starts 139/42 ends 158?	Life of Antoninus Pius	Corbridge 139 & 140 Antonine Wall 142+ Pius Imperator 142 rebuilding of Hadrian's Wall 158	special issue 142/43	
ANTONINE II (reoccupation of southern Scotland) starts 158? ends *c*. 165			coin of 164+	no samian after *c*. 163
SEVERAN (reconquest of southern Scotland as far north as the Tay) starts 208/9 ends 212+	Cassius Dio, Herodian	inscription at Carpow Feb 212+	special issue of 208	

29

CHAPTER TWO

Invasion

The nature of the Roman empire

The Roman State was an empire and its leaders were, in modern terminology, imperialists, with imperialists' attitudes to other people. They considered themselves free to interfere in the affairs of adjacent States if they perceived their own interests to be threatened. This was underpinned by a belief that they had a mission to rule the world, to bring to it the benefits of their own civilization, and they lived in an environment where there were very few equally strong States. Only Parthia (Persia) was of equal status and it is not surprising that many great Roman generals saw that country as their most challenging opponent. No other State was capable of withstanding Rome when she was at the height of her powers.

The Romans had few compunctions about dealing with their enemies. Their aim was to persuade their opponents to submit peacefully. If this failed, then military action would follow. Usually the Romans won. But in many cases the defeated rebelled and then the Romans were much more ruthless. In 77, following the revolt of the Ordovices, Tacitus states that Agricola set out to exterminate the tribe. After the Caledonians and Maeatae had been conquered in 209, both rebelled and the Roman army was ordered into the field with instructions to kill everyone it met.

In spite of the Romans' own view of their 'mission' they still liked to be able to fight a just war whenever possible, a war forced on them by the intransigence of their enemy. Thus, in 82, Agricola 'feared a rising of the northern tribes' and so moved across the Forth; only then did the enemy retaliate and 'without provocation' attack a Roman fort. Another ploy was to intervene to support one side in an internal quarrel. Claudius entered Britain in 43 to support a prince of the Atrebates while Agricola in 81 had a fugitive Irish prince in his retinue when considering an invasion of that island.

This colossal power was wielded by individual and competing nobles in the late republic. Julius Caesar invaded Gaul primarily because warfare there would allow him to extend his governorship of the neighbouring province, and when he had conquered Gaul Britain provided a new enemy. What was best for the Roman State was of no concern to him, only what was best for Caesar. Britain lost its interest to Caesar when he acquired absolute power: then his attentions turned elsewhere, to Parthia.

The invasion of Britain

The concerns of the Emperors Augustus and Tiberius also lay elsewhere but Britain suddenly returned to the agenda under their successors. Caligula appears to have contemplated a British campaign, and probably raised two new legions for the task. Britain might still have remained unconquered but for his murder in 41. His successor, Claudius, had been kept in the background by his family, apparently largely because of his physical disabilities: he had a limp and he stuttered. Unlike his famous brother, Germanicus, and his father, Drusus, he had never served in the army: indeed he had had to wait until the age of 47 before being created a senator by his nephew, Caligula. Claudius inherited the prestige of the Julio-Claudians but his personal lack of military authority was a severe disadvantage in a state which was essentially a military dictatorship (**colour plate 2**). To strengthen his position, Claudius required military prestige, and this was acknowleged by Suetonius who gave as the reason for the invasion of Britain the necessity to furnish Claudius with a triumph. While Claudius may have chosen Britain as the place to gain his prestige in order to link himself with the expoits of his famous forebear Julius Caesar, it cannot be gainsaid that the island was merely where Claudius chose to gain his military victory. The concept of a foreign political adventure in order to bolster the prestige of a ruler is not unfamiliar in today's world.

The force assembled for the invasion was substantial, four legions totalling over 20,000 men and an equivalent number of auxiliaries, or second-line troops. The four legions were *II Augusta, XIV* and *XX* from Germany and *IX Hispana* from Pannonia (modern Hungary) (**14, 15**). We know little of the auxiliary regiments which accompanied the army, but they almost certainly included Batavians from the Rhine estuary.

The Romans defeated the predominant tribe of the south-east, the Catuvellauni, in two battles but waited for the *coup de grâce*, the capture of the enemy's capital, until the arrival of the emperor. Claudius travelled by sea from Rome to Marseilles and thence across Gaul to the Channel. He spent sixteen days on the island, riding into Colchester (*Camulodunum*) at the head of his army which included several elephants. On his departure he instructed his governor, Aulus Plautius, 'to conquer the rest'.

14 *Each legion appears to have had its own emblem. That of* legio XX Valeria Victrix *was a boar.*

While Claudius and Plautius presumably understood these instructions, they are opaque to us. Did 'the rest' mean 'the rest of the island', or only what they had previously determined? Later events suggest that while the long-term aim was the conquest of the whole island – this would, after all, tie in with the Romans' view of themselves and their relationship to the world – the first stage was the conquest of the tribes of south-east Britain and their incorporation into a province.

For the first twenty-five years after the invasion the area of the province remained fairly static. It included the States of the south and midlands of modern England. Not all had the same relationship with Rome. The Iceni of East Anglia, for example, were allowed to retain their king, Prasutagus, and granted 'client' status. On the death of Prasutagus in 60 it was decided to incorporate his kingdom into the province. It was Roman brutality and rapacity at this time which led to the revolt of his widow, Boudica, and nearly resulted in the loss of the province. A further client kingdom, the Brigantes, lay to the north. This State occupied most of the territory from the Humber-Mersey line to the Tyne–Solway isthmus and possibly

15 *The ritual sacrifice at the beginning of a campaign as portrayed on the Bridgeness distance-slab from the Antonine Wall. A bull, sheep and pig await sacrifice. As this is* legio II Augusta, *the officer officiating may be Claudius Charax, the legionary legate, a native of Pergamum in Asia Minor.*

beyond. Another queen, Cartimandua, was to play an important part here. She was queen in 51 and Tacitus implies that her link with Rome went back to the time of Aulus Plautius, so she may have been queen at the time of the invasion in 43: she continued to rule until 69.

The Roman response to the expulsion of Cartimandua from her kingdom in 69 and its take-over by anti-Roman forces was the first step in an advance which, within the space of thirteen years, led to the incorporation of Wales, northern England, and southern and eastern Scotland into the province. The emperor who ordered this forward policy was Vespasian (16). He had served in the army of invasion and at the time of Nero's overthrow and suicide in 68 he was the general charged with the task of putting down the Jewish revolt in Judaea. Vespasian was the eventual victor in a civil war which saw four emperors in quick succession before peace was restored.

The governors charged by Vespasian with the task of restoring order in Britain and taking forward Roman arms were Petillius Cerialis, Sextus Julius Frontinus and Gnaeus Julius Agricola. The first conquered the Brigantes, the second the Welsh tribes, and the third north Britain. The name of Agricola is best known today, but at the time the other two were more famous. Cerialis was the general who had defeated the Batavian revolt led by Civilis in 70 and was probably a relative of the emperor. Frontinus was a consular and was to go on to hold the consulship thrice – a rare occurrence – and to write several books. There was, however, a particular factor in the choice of Agricola as governor of Britain: he was a strong supporter of the dynasty, having gone over to Vespasian's party in 69 before the would-be emperor had even publicly declared his hand. He had also served in the province twice before, as a legionary tribune during the Boudiccan revolt in 60/1 and as a legionary legate (commanding officer) in 70–3/4. For most of this latter period the governor was Petillius Cerialis so Agricola presumably

16 *The Emperor Vespasian (69–79) who ordered the first invasion of Scotland.*

gained first-hand experience of north Britain. Service in the same province at three different ranks was, as far as we know, unique and only occurred through a coincidence of circumstances, not least through Agricola's position as a friend and supporter of the imperial family. Agricola, unusually for a Roman governor, came to the province with considerable local knowledge and experience.

Agricola and the conquest of the north

Agricola returned to Britain in 77. His first action was the suppression of a revolt by the Ordovices of central and north Wales. Agricola had arrived in the province late in the season and thus the following summer, 78, was his first full campaigning season. Unfortunately Tacitus does not inform us where this occurred, and his reference to estuaries and woods is no help for this is merely a stock phrase. It is usually assumed that this season's campaign was in the territory of the Brigantes, yet this is, perhaps, unlikely for the campaign appears to have been in territory previously reconnoitred but not yet conquered, for Tacitus sums up the results of the campaign in the following manner: 'many

States which had till then maintained their independence abandoned their resentful mood and accepted the curb of garrisons and forts'. The implication is that the Romans had met these States before and this is emphasized by the reference to the 'opening up of new nations' in the following year and 'the conquest of nations hitherto unknown' in the fifth season, 82. Moreover, there is a hint in a comment by Pliny the Elder (who died on 24 August 79 in an eruption of Vesuvius) in his *Natural History*, probably written in 77, that the Roman army had already operated some distance north of the Solway, for he remarks that 'in nearly thirty years now Roman arms have extended our knowledge of it not beyond the neighbourhood of the Caledonian Forest'. Now the Caledonian Forest, we know from the later *Geography* of Ptolemy, lay beyond the Tay. Thus, it seems possible that Roman armies had actually penetrated southern Scotland even before Agricola's governorship commenced.

There are two candidates for such action. The poet Statius wrote that Vettius Bolanus, governor from 68 to 71, operated on the Caledonian plain, administering justice as well as fighting and building forts and look-out posts. Bolanus had to rescue Cartimandua from her Brigantian enemies, and we may here be seeing no more than hyperbole or inaccurate reporting.

The other candidate is Petillius Cerialis. Activity on his part north of the Solway receives support from a dendrochronological (tree-ring) date of 72/3 for the felling of wood used in the primary rampart of the fort at Carlisle. This strengthens the argument for a Cerialian foundation for the fort, originally advanced as long ago as 1913 on the basis of samian pottery.

What are the implications for Agricola? If Cerialis had planted a fort at Carlisle, he might have advanced beyond the Solway and we might also expect that his subjugation of the Brigantes was more thorough than sometimes supposed. Such an appreciation of Cerialis' activities would have left Agricola with little to do in Brigantia. Thus some or all of Agricola's second season might have been undertaken north of the Solway in southern Scotland. As he also apparently operated there during his third season, ravaging tribes as far north as the Tay, his army appears to have had a more leisurely progress than normally presumed (**table 2**).

Military decision making

Agricola's progress to the Tay, we believe, took him beyond the limits of activity of his predecessors: did he take the decision to move north himself? This seems most unlikely. Under the Roman empire it was the emperor who decided where the frontiers of the empire should lie. This is clearly shown by a wry comment made by the general Domitius Corbulo in 43 when ordered by the Emperor Claudius to withdraw behind the Rhine that 'old-time commanders were more fortunate'. Governors appear to have been sent out to their provinces with specific instructions, regularly reporting their actions to the emperor – as Tacitus records Agricola did in 77 – and receiving new instructions as appropriate. When the emperor died, the governor had to seek a new mandate from his successor. Thus when Galba became emperor in 68, Vespasian was attempting to put down the revolt of the Jews but he immediately stopped campaigning and sent to ask the new emperor for instructions.

Seventy years later, we are left in no doubt as to who ordered the second advance into Scotland. The biography of Antoninus Pius, written much later admittedly, states 'that the emperor waged many wars, using his legates. Lollius Urbicus, a legate, conquered the Britons for him....' Cornelius Fronto, the tutor of Antoninus Pius' heir, Marcus Aurelius, also gave the credit to the emperor, claiming that 'although the emperor stayed in his palace in Rome and delegated responsibility for the war, he deserved the glory for the whole start and progress of the expedition as though he had taken charge of the steering of a warship'.

Table 2 The governorship of Gnaeus Julius Agricola

year	emperor	Agricola's actions
77	Vespasian	crushed revolt of Ordovices
78	Vespasian	subdued hitherto independent States and built forts
79	Vespasian died 23 June Titus succeeded	opened up new nations; ravaged as far as Tay and built forts
80	Titus	consolidation on Forth–Clyde isthmus
81	Titus died 13 September Domitian succeeded	started with a sea passage; subdued nations hitherto unknown; considered invasion of Ireland
82	Domitian	operated north of Forth; night attack on *legio IX*
83	Domitian	battle of Mons Graupius; recall of Agricola

It is clear, too, that it was the Emperor Septimius Severus who took the decision in 208 to come to Britain and personally lead the expedition against the Caledonians and Maeatae. He was followed in the next century by three successive members of the Constantian dynasty travelling to Britain between 297 and 343.

In spite of the direct, and often close, interest of the emperor, we may presume that a governor had a certain freedom of action. Agricola will have dealt with the revolt of the Ordovices without first seeking approval from Rome. But the extension of the empire was another matter. It is interesting in this regard to consider the governorship of Agricola. It was not a smooth progress, but 'go, stop, go': the move north in 78 and 79; the halt on the Forth–Clyde line in 80 with clearly no advance the following year either; the campaigns north of the Forth in 82 and 83. These actions may be related to the wider scene. Vespasian died in June 79: the following two seasons Agricola made no significant progress; Titus died in September 81 and the following season saw Agricola moving forward again. It is hard to avoid the conclusion that these changes in emphasis were related to the changes of emperor.

The language used by Tacitus might be taken to support this interpretation. In describing Agricola's placing of forts on the Forth–Clyde isthmus in 80, Tacitus says that 'if the valour of the army and the glory of the Roman name had allowed it, a halting place would have been found within the island'. Yet, two years later Agricola moved forward; clearly the valour of the army and the glory of the Roman name had prevented him from stopping on the Forth–Clyde isthmus. But who interpreted what the valour of the army or the glory of the Roman name allowed: surely only the emperor was capable of such action? Tacitus was not prepared to allow Domitian the credit for the decision to renew the advance for by the time that the *Agricola* was written Domitian had been murdered, his memory damned, and a new emperor was at the helm (17).

At the local level, Agricola would have turned to his senior officers for advice: it was presumably some of these who recommended

17 *Coin of Domitian, the emperor (81–96) who ordered the advance beyond the Tay.*

withdrawal south of the Forth in 82 when the Caledonians attacked a Roman fort and urged him to bring up the legions from the rear immediately before the battle started at Mons Graupius. Caesar regularly included his centurions in his councils of war and we may suspect that Agricola did the same. After all, these officers were the backbone of the army, having the longest experience: and they bore the greatest casualties during fighting.

The emperor would bring his own council on campaign. Claudius brought some advisers with him in 43, though, it was said, in order to stop them plotting behind his back in Rome! Severus, too, travelled with a large retinue, and a large sum of money.

Reconnaissance

What sort of information did Agricola have to aid him when he set out to conquer the people of north Britain?

Firstly, Agricola may have had his own experience on which to draw. He had been one of Cerialis' senior officers during the conquest of the Brigantes in the early 70s. He commanded

legio XX Valeria Victrix and apparently had been given additional authority by the governor. If Cerialis had established a fort at Carlisle, or campaigned beyond, then Agricola, whose legion was generally based in western Britain, might have been there also.

Secondly, there may have been records, perhaps even official records, available to Agricola. Pytheas of Marseilles had explored the British coastline over 300 years before but his account was not believed and it is not clear how much it influenced later generations. Caesar, however, knew that Britain was an island, though he considerably underestimated its size. Mela, in the middle of the first century AD, recorded that there were 30 Orkney islands and 7 in Shetland; and he also knew of Thule (Shetland, alas, is not Thule, which lay further to the north and may have been Norway or Iceland). Pliny the Elder mentioned Pytheas' account and knew of the Caledonian Forest, the Orkney islands (his figure was 40), the Shetlands (7 islands) and the Hebrides (30 islands). These figures are not unreasonable, all things considered, but it is not clear how much of this geographical information was available to Agricola.

Claudius Ptolemaeus – Ptolemy – prepared his *Geography* in the decade 140–50 (**18** and see **6**). He included within it a considerable amount of evidence about the north of Britain, including many place-names within the area of Agricola's campaigns and information about coastal features. The most obvious time when this information could have been gathered was during Agricola's campaigns when, it might be presumed, Agricola's staff recorded geographical information for onward transmission, building on information which they themselves had to hand. This is supported by a comment by Plutarch. He remarked that in 83 Demetrius of Tarsus arrived in Delphi *en route* to his home from Britain. He had been commissioned

18 *Ptolemy's view of Scotland which owed as much to earlier explorers as to Agricola's expeditions.*

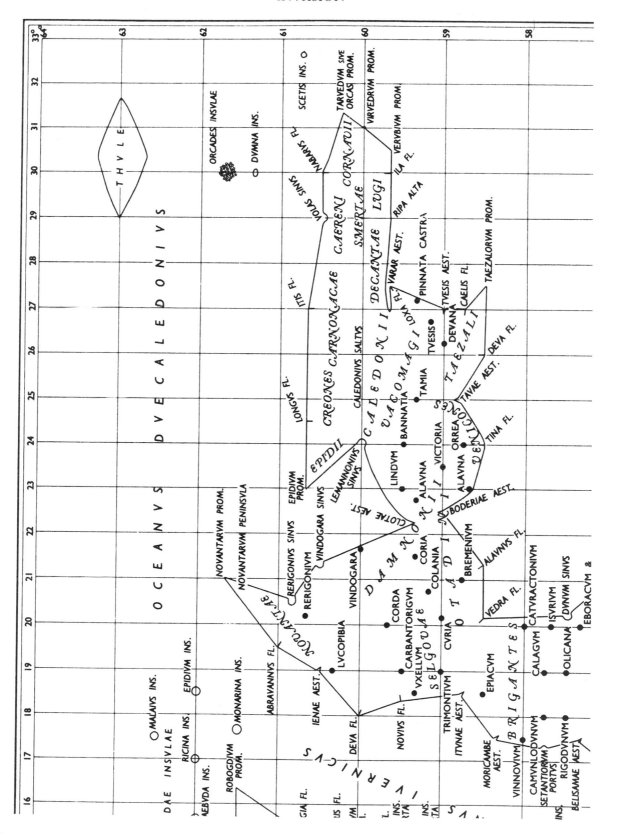

by the emperor to sail to the nearest of the islands around Britain to make enquiries and observations: it only had a few inhabitants, all were holy men who were considered sacrosanct by the Britons. The other islands were widely scattered and sparsely inhabited. It is probable that these islands were the Hebrides. Demetrius presumably was attached to Agricola's expedition: the reference indicates official interest in geographical information at the highest level. We can also presume that Demetrius would have collected the known information about the areas he explored before setting out and that therefore this information was available to Agricola.

No mapper is known in a legion, but an inscription from Rome records a mapper and engraver in the praetorian guard. And maps did exist in the Roman world. Augustus' right-hand man, Agrippa, for example, had placed a map of the world in one of his public buildings in the *Campus Martius* in Rome, while a third-century map known as *The Peutinger Table* survives in the form of a thirteenth-century copy: unfortunately the only part of Britain included is the south-east corner.

Agricola will also have relied upon local information. The Roman army generally took care to obtain as much information as possible about the land and people ahead from merchants, refugees and travellers before commencing a campaign, as Caesar and Tacitus both record.

On the march the army relied upon guides, scouts and interpreters, prisoners, deserters and no doubt friendly tribesmen. Some marches themselves were probably little more than reconnaissance expeditions. Agricola's fifth season appears to have been spent in western Scotland and it is possible that the primary purpose of the campaign was to seek a western route round the Highlands. Yet, while the land was *terra incognita* to the Romans, the locals were the descendants of people who had lived there for generations and knew their way round the area: all the

Roman army had to do was to find trustworthy guides!

Finally, while it is not possible to determine how much Agricola and his staff knew of the detailed geography of north Britain, the choice of routes for the passage of the army clearly demonstrates a grasp of the essentials of the topography of the northern countryside.

Agricola's army

The Roman army was one of the most successful fighting forces which the world has seen. In the aftermath of his victory over Mark Anthony at Actium in 31 BC, the Emperor Augustus reorganized the army. Thereafter it comprised, for most of our period, several different groups. In Rome were the praetorian guard, the urban cohorts, the fire brigade and the emperor's bodyguard. In the provinces there were two main groups, the legions and the auxiliary (literally 'helpers') units. In addition, there was the fleet, or rather fleets, for these were spread about the empire as necessity demanded.

Four legions were based in Britain and perhaps fifty or more auxiliary regiments (**colour plates 3, 4**). Each legion contained a little over 5000 men organized into cohorts, each subdivided into centuries (**19**). The commander of the legion was the legate, a senator in his mid-thirties, who normally held the post for three years. His titular deputy, the *tribunus laticlavius*, was also from the senatorial aristocracy, but usually only aged between 18 and 21. These two officers held these posts during a career in the imperial service during which civilian and military posts were interspersed. A legionary legate would often, in later years, govern a military province, as did Agricola who, as we have seen, held all three military posts in Britain.

These men were, in some ways, amateurs: it is perhaps remarkable that the Romans lost so few armies! The professional soldier was the third-in-command, the prefect of the camp.

19 *Legionaries on the march*.

Several of the small number of surviving strength reports show that regiments were often below their theoretical total, in one case by nearly 25 per cent.

The infantry were organized into centuries and the cavalry into troops. In both legions and auxiliary units the century appears to have contained only 80 men, not the 100 which the name might lead us to expect, though the evidence for numbers is slight. The cavalry troop, we believe, contained 32 men under the command of a decurion.

Agricola's army was dispersed across much of the province during the winter. His legions were based at Caerleon, Wroxeter, Chester and York while his auxiliary regiments were dotted about Wales and northern England. Each summer he had to concentrate his army before being able to take the field. Tacitus states that at the end of the season each unit returned to its winter-quarters.

Agricola is unlikely to have taken all his army on campaign. Some troops would have been required to maintain police activities within the newly conquered territory, while even during the campaigns which led to Mons Graupius, sections of the British army were serving abroad in Germany: *legio IX* was particularly below strength in 82. It was perhaps for this reason that Agricola had to use the fleet in 83 to bring his army up to strength. Thus, in spite of theoretically having about 40,000 men at his disposal, there is a real possibility that Agricola had only about half that number of soldiers with him at Mons Graupius.

For specific campaigns the army might be supplemented by special detachments. Septimius Severus brought some or all of the praetorian guard with him in 208 as well as detachments from other legions. A hundred or so years later special field armies were created in order to compensate for the immobility of the traditional army which had become fossilized on frontiers. After the Barbarian Conspiracy of 367 Count Theodosius restored

This was a man who had previously served in the centurionate and therefore often started his career in the ranks. The final group of senior officers were the junior tribunes. These were recruited from the junior aristocracy, the equestrian order. They usually held the post for about three years within a career which included command of auxiliary units.

There were as many as six different types of auxiliary units, infantry or cavalry or mixed, 500- or 1000-strong. The work-horse of the frontier was the mixed 500-strong regiment. Thousand-strong cavalry units were rare and there was never more than one in a province; the other 1000-strong units were also rare. These figures are to some extent nominal.

order with the field army from Trier, but some years later a separate field army was established in Britain itself.

Supply and logistics

Agricola's army would have had a considerable amount of equipment and food to carry with it on campaign. Various ancient writers suggest that about twenty days' supply of food for each soldier would be taken. The late first-century Jewish writer Josephus records that in addition to three days' rations each soldier carried a saw, basket, axe, pick, rope, sickle and chain. Trajan's Column shows soldiers carrying cooking vessels, a string bag and a leather satchel (**20, 21** and **colour plate 3**). In addition, entrenching tools and turf cutters (see **26**) were part of the normal equipment, as probably were artillery and medical equipment. Enormous numbers of tents were required. Soldiers slept eight to a tent and an army of 20,000 would need over 500 tents.

Not all was carried by the soldiers themselves. Mules and oxen were used to pull carts and carry tents, weapons, cooking equipment and barrels (**22**). Mules and oxen required feeding and normally no more than about ten days' supply of fodder could be carried with the army. Thereafter, additional supplies would have had to be transported to the army by land or by sea (see **72**), or local foraging undertaken.

Tacitus furnishes little evidence on how Agricola's army was supplied. On several occasions Agricola made use of his fleet – to aid the attack on Anglesey in 77, to explore in 81, to reconnoitre the harbours in 82, to harry the enemy in 83 – but nowhere is it stated that the fleet was used to supply the army. In fact warships were not suitable for conveying goods.

Caesar in his account of his wars in Gaul makes frequent reference to the need to reach a particular location by a certain date in order to collect supplies. It is clear that his campaigning was to no small extent controlled by his need to keep his army provisioned.

Agricola would have attempted, in part at least, to live off the land. Trajan's Column shows soldiers harvesting corn (**23**) and Caesar's army in southern Britain in 55 BC had been caught while foraging in the fields. Yet

20 *This cooking pot, or* patera, *found at Dowalton, in south-west Scotland, would have been carried by a Roman soldier. It was made in Italy in the first century by P. Cipius Polibius.*

21 *A soldier's water flask found at Newstead. Made of iron with bronze fittings, this is extremely rare.*

crops would not be ready to harvest until late summer so alternative means of supply had to be used before then. Caesar raided villages in order to obtain local stores of grain. Roman soldiers, however, did not just eat food such as bread, porridge or gruel made from grain, but had a more varied diet. Local farms would have provided cattle and sheep, for example. Polybius, in his description of a Roman camp, assigned a place to cattle. Firewood would also have been obtained locally, as would water, a commodity in plentiful supply in north Britain.

There is no reason to assume that Agricola's army would not have been able to forage during the course of its marches through north Britain. People had been living there for 8000 years. During that time much of the area, particularly the more fertile land of the eastern lowlands, had been denuded of trees: pollen analysis in the vicinity of the Antonine Wall, for example, has shown that the tree cover during the Roman period was probably about the same as today. Tacitus and later writers describe the Roman armies as traversing woods and marshes, but such comments are merely stock phrases, and should not be taken altogether seriously (see 5).

22 *Carts carrying supplies pulled by oxen and mules.*

23 *A legionary cutting corn.*

The whole of the countryside traversed by Agricola's army was occupied by farms where cattle and sheep and perhaps some pigs were reared, and crops such as wheat and barley grown (**colour plate 16**). The use of turf for the construction of fort ramparts indicates the existence of large areas of pasture: clearly marching-camps were laid out over open country. Marshes are a different matter. There must have been much more marshland then. Much land which is dry farmland today was only drained in the eighteenth century.

The requirements of an army the size of Agricola's were enormous. In order for it to move, considerable numbers of mules, oxen and horses would have been required and the complement continually maintained. By 16, after two campaigns in Germany, Germanicus had exhausted the supply of horses in Gaul. The fact that Agricola was able to take the field each year is eloquent testimony to the army's organizing ability.

On the march

Having assembled his force and determined his route Agricola set out (see **19**). The army itself would be spread across the country for many miles. A force of 20,000 men with its slaves and camp-followers might extend to 16km (10 miles) if kept as a single group – in 82 Agricola divided his army into three groups. The Emperor Julian's army of 30,000 during the Persian campaign of 363 was 6.5km (4 miles) long when drawn up ready to march at the beginning of the day, but extended over 16km (10 miles) on the march.

Agricola's army would have marched in a set order. One of the most comprehensive descriptions of a Roman army on the march is given by Agricola's contemporary, the Jewish writer Josephus. He recorded that skirmishers or lightly armed troops were sent ahead. Towards the front of the main force marched the surveyors and engineers. Following these were the carriages of the officers and the senior officers themselves, all protected by a special guard. Next came the legionary cavalry and then the artillery train. The commanding officers of the auxiliary regiments had their own bodyguard. The legions, the soldiers arranged six abreast, marched one after the other.

24 *Aerial photograph of the temporary camp at Pennymuir. The entrances on each side can be seen clearly. A smaller camp lies in the corner of the main camp.*

25 *A tent peg and mallet (the haft and rope are modern) found at Newstead.*

attacked at night but managed to defend itself until reinforcements arrived.

Within each camp, the tents were arranged in rows following set plans. Surveyors travelling with the advance guard marked the lines ready for the soldiers to pitch the tents (**25, 26, 27**). The position of the officers and the individual units were known to all so that in the event of attack each soldier automatically knew where to go. Wide streets crossed the camp and also ran round the circuit inside the rampart: here sorties could assemble before charging out through the entrances.

Camps were the most ephemeral of Roman military remains, often occupied for only one or two nights. A later Byzantine writer points out that no army should stay longer than three nights in any one place for in that time it would have eaten all the food in the area and fouled its own water supply.

Scrvants led the baggage train and at the rear was a strong force of infantry and cavalry. Cavalry might also be employed in the van or on the flanks.

Each night that thc army stopped it protected itself by constructing a camp, a relatively light defence, but nevertheless important (**24**). The whole army was protected by the digging of a single ditch, at least 1.5m (5ft) wide by 0.90m (3ft) deep according to a surviving military manual, and the heaping of the material inside to form a mound: wooden stakes – each soldier carried two – were stuck into the top of the rampart to strengthen it. Wide entrances were placed on each side, but were protected by detached sections of rampart and ditch, or, sometimes, curving sections of rampart and ditch. Grooves across some entrances suggest that hurdles may occasionally have been used to protect these vulnerable points. The importance of temporary camps was shown in 82 when the *legio IX* was

26 *A turf cutter found at Newstead.*

27 *Camps on Trajan's Column. Tents are clearly visible top left. In the foreground legionaries dig ditches, observed by an auxiliary soldier.*

Southern Scotland

In his third season Agricola 'opened up new nations', ravaging the territory of tribes as far as the estuary of the Tay. Ptolemy's *Geography* records the names of the tribes of southern Scotland, presumably those encountered during this season (**28** and see **18**). The Votadini occupied the east coast from Northumberland to the Forth, with the Selgovae in central-southern Scotland and the Novantae in the south-west, while the Damnonii stretched from Ayrshire into Strathearn. Several place-names are listed in each tribe, some native, others clearly Roman forts. The latter included *Bremenium* (High Rochester) in the territory of the Votadini, and, in Selgovia, *Trimontium* (Newstead) by the three Eildon Hills. In the native category are a number of places called *Coria*. 'Coria' means meeting- or hosting-place and suggests the location of the capital, or at least a chief town, of the tribe.

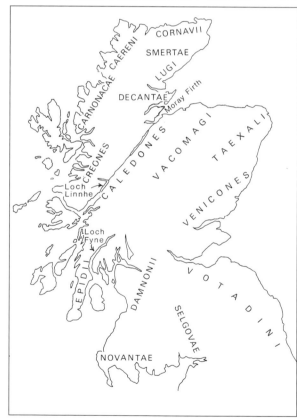

28 *The tribes of Scotland according to Ptolemy.*

Tacitus states in his account of this season that the tribes of southern Scotland did not attack the army: indeed, Agricola even had time to build forts. Some tribes may have submitted without fighting; some may have submitted in advance of the arrival of the army. However, as Agricola may have operated in this area the previous season, and he certainly spent the next year consolidating his conquests, he may have spent as long as three seasons in southern Scotland. Part of that time may not only have been spent building forts but arranging the administration of the new extension to the province.

Tacitus tells us nothing about Agricola's route. However, the discovery of marching-camps indicates the two main lines of penetration into Scotland used by the Roman army and it is probable that Agricola used one or both of these. The eastern route was that followed today by the A68; the western follows the modern A74 through Annandale and Clydesdale. This western line is a natural route, utilizing river valleys, but the eastern strikes across country which implies more knowledge of the terrain, presumably the tapping of local information by the army. Certainly the coast was sensibly avoided on the east for it is much broken by river valleys.

The Caledonians

Agricola's final two seasons, his sixth in 82 and his seventh in 83, were spent fighting the Caledonians north of the Forth. Tacitus is reticent on the details. 82 commenced with 'a general rising of the northern nations and threatening movements by the enemy on land' leading Agricola to send his fleet ahead to reconnoitre. Following Agricola's advance, the Caledonians 'without provocation' attacked a Roman fort, leading to a call for retreat. In the face of a strong and mobile enemy, Agricola divided his army into three columns, then nearly lost one, *legio IX*, when it was attacked at night: it was saved by its camp defences and

the timely arrival of the rest of the army. A further set-back was the mutiny of a recently raised regiment which seized three warships.

There are even fewer details recorded about the final campaign. The fleet was again used, the army marched light and achieved victory, late in the season, probably September, at Mons Graupius. Thereafter, Agricola led his army into the territory of the Boresti, an otherwise unknown tribe, where he took hostages, returning thence through the territory of fresh nations, while he sent his navy to circumnavigate Britain: on the voyage it subdued the Orkney islands and sighted land beyond which it thought was Thule.

Tacitus gives no precise routes, nor does he locate Mons Graupius: we cannot even be certain where the Caledones lived (see **28**). Ptolemy records that their territory stretched from the Lemannonian Gulf on the west coast (probably Loch Long, Loch Fyne or Loch Linnhe) to the Varar estuary on the east (Beauly Firth). The shortest line between these two points is the Great Glen, but there is relatively little settlement known there, insufficient to support an army 30,000-strong. Accordingly it has been suggested that the Caledones' territory stretched round the south and east sides of the Highland massif, where the modern place-names of Dunkeld, Schiehallion and Rohallion are all derived from Caledonia or Caledones. This location would include Strathmore, which today contains some of Scotland's richest farmland.

However, while Ptolemy lists the Caledones among his tribes, Tacitus never specifically refers to such a tribe. He writes of Caledonia and the inhabitants of Caledonia. To him, Caledonia was a place containing several tribes. Perhaps the Caledones were the largest tribe north of the Forth and had given their name to the area.

In spite of these uncertainties, it is clear from all sources that Caledonia and the Caledones lay north of the Forth. That is a considerable swathe of territory. Marching-camps can, however, help locate Agricola's campaigns within that area (**29**). An early, and

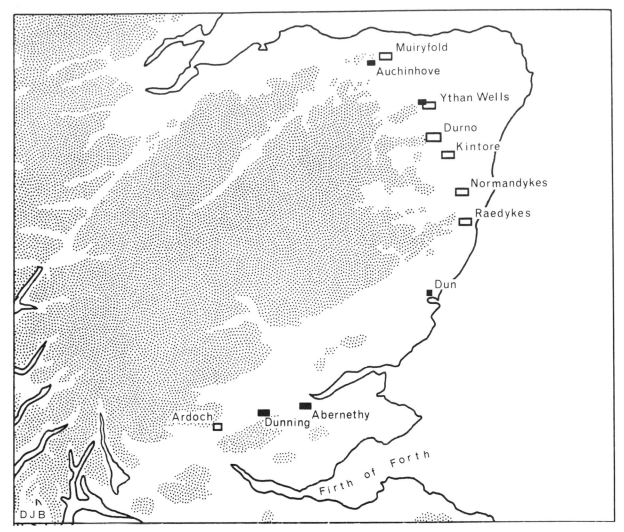

29 *Camps in Scotland considered to date to the campaigns of Agricola.*

therefore probably Agricolan, series of camps has been recognized in eastern Scotland, extending northwards through Strathmore and beyond the Mounth, possibly as far north as Auchinhove in Aberdeenshire. These seem to indicate the main focus of Agricola's activities.

Yet there ought to be many more camps. In 82 the army was divided into three groups, while in 83 it may have been in the field for some considerable time for Mons Graupius was not fought until 'the season was nearly over'. The campaigning season started in mid-March, though Agricola may not have gone into the field until mid-May when the grass would have started to grow. This would have allowed four or five months between the start of the campaign and the battle. It is not clear what Agricola was doing for those months: a march to and from the northernmost known camp would only have taken about two months.

Assistance may come from another source. Much of the information in Ptolemy's *Geography* pertaining to the north of Britain, it is generally agreed, was acquired during Agricola's campaigns. The information is not uniformly spread across the north: there are no place-names listed north and west of the Great Glen, for example. This suggests that Agricola's army did not penetrate into these areas. There are, however, place-names on a line stretching roughly south-south-west from the mouth of the Spey (see **18**). This line closely follows the line of the river and may suggest that the army reconnoitred this strath – or perhaps even returned to the province along this route after Mons Graupius. As a result of the heavily wooded nature of Strathspey it will be difficult to locate marching-camps here.

Mons Graupius

The culmination of the *Agricola* is the battle of Mons Graupius. This was certainly the pinnacle of Agricola's achievements, and the book was written in order to lead the narrative on to that event. Details could be ignored, while the text is sprinkled with literary phrases which implicitly compare Agricola with great generals: the crossing of estuaries and woods, defeating 'unknown' nations, choosing the location of camp-sites himself, were all the attributes of a good general (and were used of Severus later). The manner in which the book is written, however, should not cloud us to Agricola's achievement in defeating the Caledonians.

There have been many attempts to locate the battle but in truth we are little closer now than was General Roy 200 years ago. The northern-most marching-camps near Huntly are a pointer, and so is the terrain. Professor St Joseph argued that the hill now known as Bennachie, with the camp at Durno (see **29**) near its base, was the correct site. An alternative in the same area favoured by some is Knock Hill. Sir Ian Richmond, drawing on human geography, suggested that a location near Culloden would be suitable, for this is the last point at which the Highland tribes or clans can make a stand before their armies melt away up the various glens leading north, west and south from the Moray Firth. Other commentators have prefered philology and suggested links between Roman and modern place-names. This led Richard Feachem to propose Dunning as the site. We remain, however, uncertain of the correct location. All we know is what Tacitus tells us.

In September 83 the Roman army arrived at Mons Graupius, the Graupian Mountain, which it found occupied by 'the full force of all' the north British States, 30,000 men, assembled under the leadership of Calgacus. Tacitus does not inform us of the size of Agricola's army, but he does say that the enemy had a 'great superiority in numbers'. This might imply a relationship of 2:1. Agricola certainly had 8000 auxiliaries and probably 5000 cavalry together with legionaries. The number of legionaries is nowhere mentioned, but it is unlikely to have been as few as 2000. Seven–eight thousand legionaries, rather less than two complete legions, would give parity with the auxiliary infantry and a total force of about 20,000. The relationship then would be 3:2, perhaps sufficiently far apart to allow use of the phrase 'great superiority in numbers', though a legionary strength of 5000 or even 4000 may be nearer the mark.

In making his dispositions, Agricola placed the auxiliary infantry, 8000 in number, in the centre, with the ranks spread out in the face of the stronger force, and 3000 cavalry on the flanks. The legions were in the rear, drawn up in front of the camp, together with about 2000 cavalry. They faced the Caledonians drawn up in tiers on the gentle slope with its van on the level ground (**colour plate 1**).

Before the battle, the Caledonian chariots raced across the ground between the two armies, to be routed by the Roman cavalry. The battle started with an exchange of missiles followed by the Roman advance up the slope. At close quarters, the short Roman sword was at an advantage over the longer slashing sword of the Caledonians, while the auxiliaries also used their larger shields as a weapon (**30**). The Roman infantry was initially successful and was joined by the cavalry. The sheer numbers of the Caledonians combined with the roughness of the ground halted this advance and gradually the Romans began to be outflanked.

30 *This auxiliary soldier wields his shield as a weapon. His spear, rendered in metal on the Column and now lost, was held in his right hand; the sword is still in its sheath.*

In a counter-move Agricola sent in his reserve cavalry, who stemmed the flanking movement and then, in turn, fell on the rear of the Caledonian infantry (**31**). The Caledonians broke and, as usual, most casualties were suffered in flight: 10,000 are said to have died against 360 Roman losses. Even taking shelter in the woods failed to save the Caledonians for Agricola dismounted his cavalry and scoured the woods on foot.

Mons Graupius was both the culmination and termination of Agricola's governorship.

Tacitus' subsequent comments are brief: the enemy was hunted down, but night prevented more bloodshed. The army, as we have seen, returned to winter-quarters. Agricola himself shortly afterwards returned to Rome.

Tacitus provides us with one of the most detailed descriptions of a battle fought on British soil during the Roman period. The tactics were relatively simple and the Romans won as a result of their superior discipline, weapons and armour. The Caledonians were disadvantaged in every way. They carried swords, spears and shields, but were not equipped with armour

31 *The Roman cavalryman on the Bridgeness distance-slab rides down four barbarians. This a typical depiction of Roman triumph.*

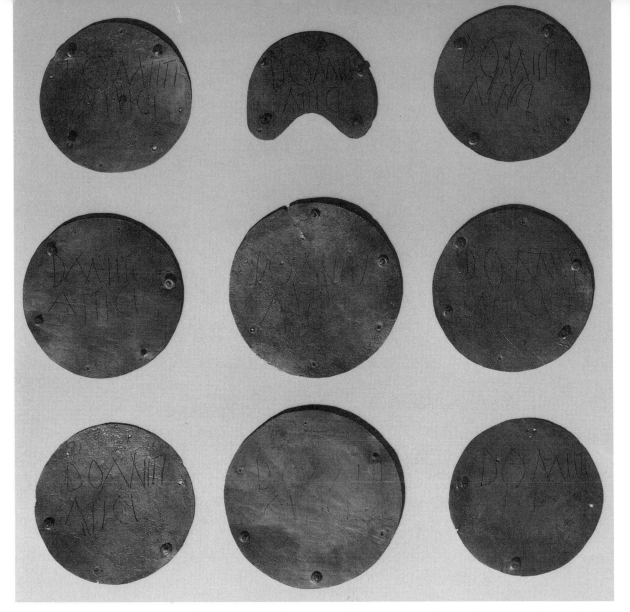

32 *Bronze back plates for* phalerae *(a type of medal) awarded to Domitius Atticus and found at Newstead.*

comparable to that worn by the Romans. It is possible that they wore no body armour at all: some Celts fought naked. The Caledonians were also using obsolete military machinery: the chariot as a vehicle of war had been abandoned elsewhere in western Europe. Finally, the Caledonians were not familiar with the discipline displayed by the Roman army. Their tactics appear to have been the same as the Highland clans of later years who attempted to win through a ferocious downhill charge.

There was indeed almost an inevitability about the result. The Britons were rarely successful in a set-piece battle against the Romans. Their best strategy was to pursue guerrilla warfare, and indeed they did undertake such activity on several occasions, for example during the Severan campaigns, when Dio records that the enemy used sheep and cattle to lure the Romans on. Yet guerrilla warfare was not successful against a ruthless foe without outside help. The Caledonians were faced by a formidable enemy and were only saved by circumstances beyond their control, as we will see.

Victory

After victory, there would have been a formal surrender of the enemy. Tacitus records no such action after Mons Graupius, but Severus and Caracalla received the surrender of the Caledonians and Maeatae in the field with the two armies drawn up facing each other.

After victory, too, thanks would have been delivered to the gods, and medals and honours dispensed to the soldiers and their commanders. The medals were issued according to rank, with the exception of the highest awards (32). Agricola, on his return to Rome, received the equivalent of a triumph.

At the end of a campaign whole regiments might be honoured for meritorious conduct. *Cohors I Cugernorum* was awarded the title *Ulpia Traiana* between 103 and 122, probably as a result of warfare in Britain. During the reign of Antoninus Pius *cohors I Baetasiorum* acquired the title *civium Romanorum*, indicating that all the soldiers in the regiment had been given Roman citizenship, a distinction normally only awarded on retirement. This may have been as a result of action during the invasion of Scotland in 139–42, when it seems probable that *cohors I Hispanorum* was awarded the use of the imperial name *Aelia*. Following the first successful campaign against the Caledonians and Maeatae in 209 *legio VI Victrix* was rewarded with the title *Britannica*.

The emperor himself might acknowledge the success of his armies. In 142 Antoninus Pius took the title *imperator*, 'Conqueror', while

33 *An eighteenth-century drawing of Arthur's O'on. This was probably a Roman victory monument; it was destroyed in 1743.*

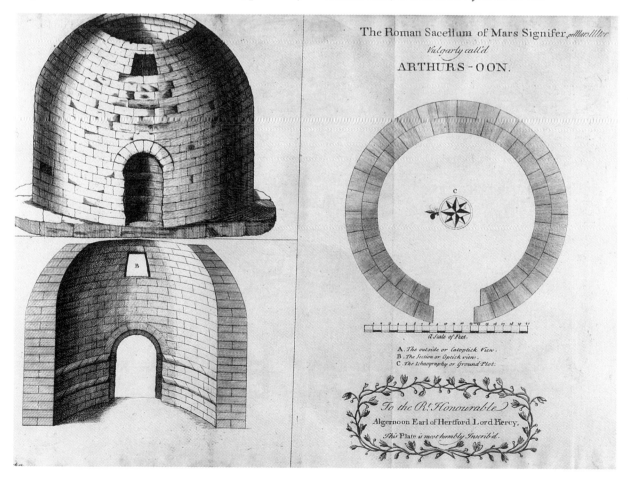

The Roman Sacellum of Mars Signifer, or Mars Ultor

Vulgarly call'd

ARThurs - OON.

A. The outside or Catoptick View.
B. The Section or Optick view.
C. The Ichnography or Ground Plot.

To the R.t Honourable

Algernoon Earl of Hertford Lord Percy,

This Plate is most humbly Inscrib'd.

34 *This finely carved head, dating to the early second century, was found at Hawkshaw, Tweedsmuir, Peeblesshire. It has been suggested that it once formed part of a monument erected to commemorate the Roman conquest.*

Severus added *Britannicus* to his many honours in 210. Sometimes the addition of *Britannicus* to an emperor's titles is the only indication of activity in Britain. A special coin issue might be struck to mark the victory (see **4**).

After victory a monument might be erected. After the conquest of Britain in 43, Claudius erected a triumphal arch in Rome and, in Britain, a great monument at Richborough, the main entry point. It seems possible that a monument was erected at the east end of Hadrian's Wall after the completion of that building project. A little to the north of the Antonine Wall, a circular domed structure known as Arthur's O'on (oven) has been interpreted as a victory monument to the successful reconquest of southern Scotland and the construction of the Wall (**33, 34**).

CHAPTER THREE

Conquest

It is too easy to assume that the Roman empire was static and unchanging. In fact it continually developed and adapted to new circumstances. Yet there were certain underlying verities. In considering the Roman army, its campaigning tactics remained broadly similar from Caesar through Agricola and into the next century. The aim was to subdue the enemy and ensure that it sued for peace. There was no attempt to gain strips of territory on the line of World War I trench fighting. If expansion was the aim, whole States or tribes would be incorporated into the empire. Physical occupation of their land by the army was not a necessity. Hostages might ensure submission to the will of Rome, and both Caesar and Agricola, for example, followed that practice in dealing with enemies during campaigning. States could be cowed by the mere threat of Roman force. The presence of Roman forts, on the other hand, did not necessarily imply hostility on the part of the host State or tribe: their land might have been friendly territory providing safe bases for Roman forces.

The pattern of control

By the time that Agricola invaded Scotland, a pattern of control had been developed which was to continue throughout the remainder of the period of Roman Britain. The legions of the province were placed some distance back from the frontier, with the newly conquered tribes controlled by a network of forts housing auxiliary regiments whose duties included protecting the new provincials from attack. As new tribes were conquered, the older forts were abandoned and the regiments moved forward.

The first task, however, was the defeat of the enemy. Tacitus, commenting on Agricola's third season in 79, when he ravaged as far as the Tay, states that he 'even had time to build forts'. The clear implication is that normally this would be left to a later season, but that in this particular year the conquest of the enemy was so easy that Agricola was able to start this work. Fort building presumably continued into the next season when the army consolidated its hold on the land up to the Forth–Clyde line.

The pattern of occupation at this time, and also in the mid-second century, was for forts or fortlets to be placed about a day's march apart, some 22km (14 miles). The larger forts tended to be placed in the main river valleys. In the late first century the largest auxiliary fort in Scotland was Newstead in the Tweed valley, with other large forts at Milton in Annandale, Dalswinton in Nithsdale, Glenlochar in the Ken valley and Castledykes in Clydesdale, while Camelon lay on the River Carron in the Forth basin (see **38**). Several of these bases were sufficiently large to hold more than one regiment. Between them were forts for single auxiliary regiments or fortlets for only eighty men or so. In the second century (see **88**) Newstead remained a major base, but the other large forts were replaced by smaller successors while fortlets appear to have been utilized in greater numbers (**colour plate 6**). The soldiers to man these fortlets were drawn from adjacent forts.

These forts and fortlets were connected by metalled all-weather roads (**colour plate 5**) and presumably native tracks were also used though we know nothing of these.

Fort building

The Roman army constructed the forts and fortlets itself (**35**). All surviving evidence supports this conclusion, though Tacitus has Calgacus say in his speech before Mons Graupius that the Romans forced the Britons to build roads through woods and swamps. Formal inscriptions record the construction of military buildings, forts and frontiers by the army (**36** and see **7**); informal doodles in quarries indicate the cutting of stone by the soldiers themselves. Inscriptions, military documents and literary sources also demonstrate that the army contained many craftsmen. Finally, sculpture such as Trajan's Column shows soldiers at work building (see **35**). The Vindolanda writing tablets provide the most recent evidence. One document records that 30 men were sent with Marcus, the medical orderly, to build the residence; 19 to burn stone; others to produce clay for the wattle fences of the camp. Another mentions lead, kilns, clay and plasterers.

The first forts were built of timber with turf ramparts and so could be constructed relatively quickly: stone was usually only used when these early buildings were replaced. Wherever possible the army liked to use long-lasting timber such as oak. In north Britain, however, the woodland had been so much reduced in extent that oak was often not available. Alder, birch, elm and hazel, therefore, were all used (**37**).

The walls of buildings were of wattle and daub. Willow was a good timber for the wattles and after clay had been applied and plastered the building was almost indistinguishable from a stone construction. What might betray its materials was the nature of the roof. This would usually be of thatch or shingles. These

35 *Legionaries building a fort. Carpenters work on the gate while other soldiers dig the ditches. Visible at the top is a soldier being relieved of his burden of a turf for the rampart.*

36 *This simple inscription records that Bearsden fort was built by* legio XX Valeria Victrix.

military buildings, therefore, were not unsophisticated. Scenes from mythology were painted on barrack-room walls in Germany.

The fort buildings were defended by a rampart of turf (see **26**). The turf might sit on a corduroy base of logs, or be revetted, possibly front and back, by a stone kerb. It is probable that there was a breastwork along the top of the rampart. One certainly existed on the stone fort of the praetorian guard built in Rome under Tiberius, and they do appear on Trajan's Column. At the second-century fort at Bearsden on the Antonine Wall, burnt wattles, mainly of willow, were found in front of the east rampart of the fort. It is possible that these are the remains of the fort's timber breastwork thrown down and burnt when the site was abandoned (see **83**).

North of the Forth

If military deployment south of the Forth–Clyde isthmus in both the late first and mid-second centuries was broadly similar, the pattern of occupation north of the Forth in all three phases of conquest was different.

It is difficult to be certain of Roman intentions regarding the land north of the Forth in the late first century for it seems likely that the network of forts was never completed. This is most clearly demonstrated by the legionary fortress at Inchtuthil (see **39**). This was abandoned in 87/8 before all its buildings had been constructed. There are two phases in the labour camps outside the fortress and also two phases in the defences: a stone wall was added to the earlier turf rampart. Inchtuthil has produced several coins of 86 and only one possible coin of 87. If the two phases in the labour camps and fortress relate to two seasons of building, then it seems most likely that the construction of Inchtuthil did not commence until after the victory had been won at Mons Graupius in 83. It is doubtful if any of the forts beyond the Tay had been constructed during either the sixth or seventh season when the army was still in the field: this would merely have led to the dissipation of Agricola's forces. As forts were normally only constructed after the defeat of the enemy it seems best to assume that they were all built after the battle.

The surviving pattern of forts north of the Forth–Clyde isthmus is interesting (**38**). They

37 *Carpenters' tools found at Newstead. They include a saw, axe, auger, chisel, file, compasses and two blades of planes.*

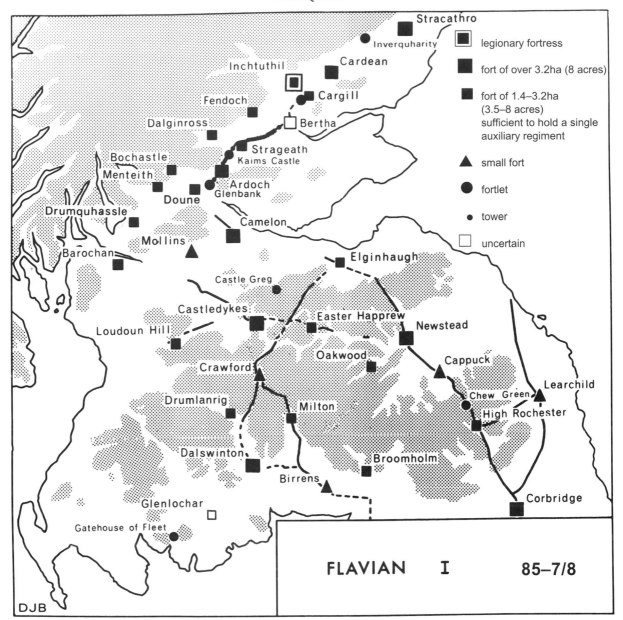

38 *Military deployment in Scotland in the late first century.*

were arrayed, broadly speaking, in two lines. One hugged the edge of the Highlands, the other ran through the more open country of the main river valleys.

The Highland Line forts are sometimes called the glen-blocking forts, an apt description of their location for many were placed in the mouths of the principal glens. The chain of forts stretched from Drumquhassle, near Drymen, perched on the high ground overlooking the southern reaches of Loch Lomond, north-eastwards to the fortlet at Inverquharity. The location of the forts at Bochastle by Callander, Dalginross near Comrie and Fendoch in the Sma' Glen is particularly interesting, for each is placed in the very mouth of the glen before it narrows and fully enters the Highlands.

Most of the second line of forts lay along a road which left the isthmus at Camelon, headed upstream to cross the Forth, or rather the Teith, at Doune, then turned northwards, passing Ardoch and Strageath *en route* to Bertha on the Tay. Beyond here forts are known at Cardean near Meigle and Stracathro near Edzell in Strathmore. The long gap between these two sites suggests that a third remains to be discovered between them. The road forts themselves fall into two groups. The more southerly exhibit two structural phases and the earlier phase may date to 79 or 80 following Agricola's march to the Tay. Possibly one of these forts was that attacked by the Caledonians in 82.

All the forts were of a size to hold auxiliary regiments – perhaps more than one in some cases. In both lines, the size of the forts varied but they appear to have been arranged in an alternating pattern of large and small installations. The small forts were about 1.6–2ha (4–5 acres) in extent, the larger ones 2.4–3.2ha (6–8 acres).

One fort, or rather fortress, Inchtuthil, is considerably larger than the rest and was built for a different unit, a complete legion (39). It lay on the River Tay, by the Dunkeld Gorge, and beside the modern A9, one of the main routes through the Highlands today. The northerly location of the fortress hints that the Romans may have intended to construct more forts beyond Inchtuthil, perhaps in the Highlands themselves. In this scenario the Highland Line forts were not glen-blocking forts but the springboards for an advance up the glens, an advance which never materialized because the linchpin of the proposals, the legionary base at Inchtuthil, had to be abandoned before its completion.

The more usual interpretation of the glen forts is that they were located to guard the exit points from the Highlands and protect the province from attack. However, few people lived in the Highlands at that time and it seems unlikely that the Romans would not have known this. People had lived in north Britain for 8000 years. Trade or exchange between groups of people had been underway for at least half that period. It is hard

to believe that the Romans would not have availed themselves of information from local people. Indeed, they may have explored the glens themselves, as the possible location of place-names in Strathspey may suggest.

Hoping to cast light on Roman intentions, archaeologists have sought forts beyond Strathmore along the Moray Firth. Several possibilities have been examined, but none to date has gained general acceptance in view of the lack of positive Roman dating evidence. The most northerly accepted fort remains Stracathro near Edzell. If the presence of the legion at Inchtuthil cannot be taken as an argument for an intention to occupy the Highlands, perhaps we should see its location as merely governed by the topography of the area. The Romans may have seen Strathtay as the most convenient position for the legionary fortress, a decision echoed by the construction of the Severan legionary base at Carpow lower down the valley 100 years later.

The failure to complete the pattern of occupation north of the Forth in the late first century makes it difficult for us to understand both the pattern and Rome's intentions. We are informed by a contemporary what Severus' intentions were over 100 years later – the conquest of the island – but not how he intended to maintain control thereafter. The only certainly known fort of that time in Scotland was Carpow. This covered 12ha (30 acres) and it seems possible that it was proposed to base detachments of two legions here: at least, two legions are recorded undertaking its construction. Presumably other forts were intended: both Dio and Herodian mention the abandonment of forts after Severus' death. One of these forts may have been at Cramond on the Forth, for third-century pottery has been found there.

The intended disposition of Roman forces north of the Forth in the late first century and the early third century may elude us, but the second-century arrangements seem clear (see 88). These, however, were limited in scope and appear to have been little more than a screen

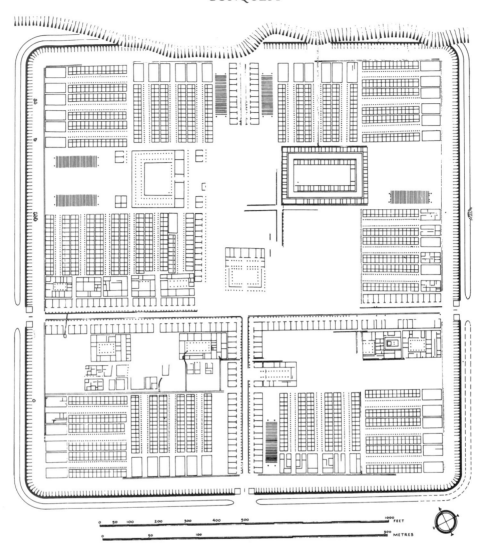

39 *Plan of the legionary fortress at Inchtuthil. The open spaces demonstrate that the fortress was never completed. Among the buildings not constructed were granaries for some of the cohorts.*

of forts placed along the road running north from the Antonine Wall to Bertha on the Tay. The Antonine Wall is, in fact, the chief difference between the three periods for at this time the Romans seem to have had limited aims and had no intention of attempting to occupy any land north of the Tay.

The Antonine Wall was not the first frontier across the Forth–Clyde isthmus. In his fourth season, as we have seen, Agricola placed a chain of garrisons across the Forth–Clyde isthmus. These installations have proved difficult to rediscover. Pottery and coins have been found beneath some of the Antonine Wall forts but structures there have been more elusive to the spade. The only known structures which may be assigned to this period are off the line of the Antonine Wall, though only just in the case of Camelon. This site was clearly one of the nodal points of Roman activity for forts of several periods lay here with six or more temporary camps adjacent. Excavations at the site produced some of the earliest Roman pottery to have been found in Scotland which points to an Agricolan foundation. At the west end of the isthmus, Barochan, on a ridge overlooking the Clyde, also dates to the first century and is a candidate for Agricola's Forth–Clyde chain of garrisons. In between only the small fort at Mollins is known. These sites, by themselves, can hardly be termed a frontier system.

There was, however, a string of posts further north, which do appear to be part of a frontier (40). A number of timber towers have long been known to lie on either side of the Roman road running along the Gask Ridge west of Perth (41). Continued reconnaissance has increased both their number and extent. They are now known to extend from a little south of Ardoch as far as the east end of the Gask Ridge. The distance between them varied but was perhaps intended to be about 0.8km (half a mile). This is too close for signalling purposes and has led to the suggestion that they formed part of a frontier. In that case, the tow-

ers would have provided elevated vantage points for soldiers so that they could observe the movement of people into and out of the province. Such movement on other frontiers was governed by regulations and there is no reason to believe that Britain was any different. Travellers could only enter the empire unarmed, under guard, by day, at fixed points and times, and upon payment. Customs dues were also payable at the frontier.

The towers did not stand alone. The road connected the forts from Camelon to Bertha, and also along it lay two fortlets. One, long known, is Kaimes Castle between Ardoch and Strageath. More interestingly, it forms part of a series of evenly spaced sites running north from Ardoch. The spacing between the north gate of the fort, the towers and the fortlet is

40 *Military dispositions along the Gask Ridge.*

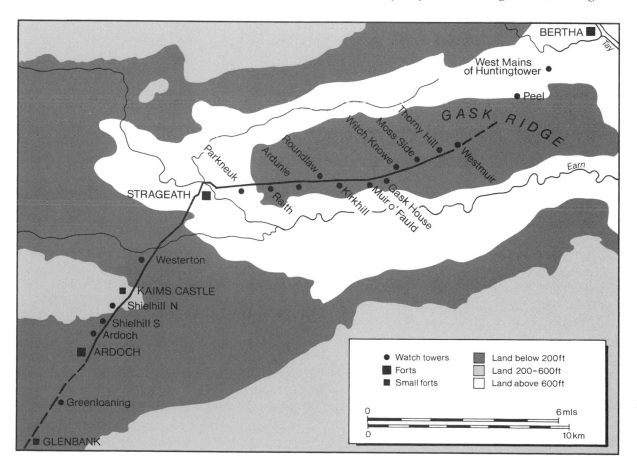

41 *An artist's impression of a tower on the Gask Ridge. Drawn by Michael J. Moore.*

1000m (3280ft) in each case. This implies a planned system, a theory further supported by the recent discovery of a second fortlet equidistant south of Ardoch.

We have no evidence that our discoveries are all that there is to be found: indeed it is highly unlikely that they are. Thus again we are trying to make sense of a jigsaw with many of the pieces missing. It is possible that the line extends up to the Tay, perhaps beyond. Its southern limit is equally interesting. Was it the Forth?

The date of this frontier system is also of interest. Over ten towers and both the fortlets have been examined, but the amount of surviving dating evidence is pitifully small. It consists of no more than three sherds of pottery, but all point to a first-century date. But when in the first century? Some archaeologists, noting that Agricola's line of garrisons lay across the Forth–Clyde and that otherwise Agricola was clearly intent on expanding the province, have

assigned the construction of the frontier system to later years, envisaging it as a stage in the withdrawal which commenced with the abandonment of Inchtuthil. However, now we can see that all the installations north of the Forth must have been built and abandoned within the period 79–88 at the outside, that scenario no longer seems possible. Yet it remains unlikely that the towers were in use while Inchtuthil was occupied, for the fortress lies to their north. If they have to be fitted into a period before the construction of the legionary fortress, then Agricola's fourth season when he consolidated his hold on southern Scotland and fortified the Forth–Clyde line might seem the best choice.

The construction of a frontier system in north Britain in the 80s, perhaps the early 80s, is interesting for it is almost exactly contemporary with similar works in Germany. The Romans are known to have erected towers earlier, but these two series appear to have been the first integrated frontier systems of a new line of development in frontier installations. They mark a distinct phase in the fossilization of the Roman empire. The empire was to continue expanding, or trying to expand, for many years, certainly up to the time of Severus. Progress was haphazard, but then it always had been, apart from during the remarkable reign of Augustus. Now, however, progress was accompanied by attempts to create systems of frontier control so that a tension was created between the periodic attempts at expansion and the construction of solid boundaries to the empire apparently intended to be permanent. The governorship of Agricola illustrates this neatly for he considerably expanded the province yet at the same time he, or his emperor, considered the establishment of a permanent boundary to that province within the island.

Hadrian's Wall

Roman frontiers were to find their most famous expression in Hadrian's Wall. The Emperor Hadrian came to Britain in 122 and, according to his biographer, 'put many things to right and was the first to build a wall, 80 miles long from sea to sea, to divide the barbarians from the Romans'. The line chosen for Hadrian's Wall lay a little to the north of an existing line of forts along the road known as the Stanegate. This road had been constructed in the first century to link Corbridge on Dere Street, the great arterial route up the eastern side of the country, with Carlisle on the western route north. Forts are known west of Carlisle and one east of Corbridge, but we cannot point to the existence of a frontier system across the Tyne–Solway isthmus prior to the construction of the Wall.

Hadrian's Wall is today entirely of stone (**42**), but the original intention was to build a stone wall, 10 Roman feet (3m) wide and perhaps 15 (4.5m) high, from Newcastle for 72km (45 miles) to the River Irthing, and a turf wall, 20 Roman feet (6m) wide, thence to Bowness. At regular mile (1.6km) intervals were gates through this barrier guarded by fortlets, which we call milecastles, each housing a small number of soldiers (8 or 32, so far as we can determine). Between each pair of milecastles were two towers or turrets, about a third of a mile (0.5km) apart therefore. This line of fortlets and towers continued westwards down the Cumbrian coast for at least 32km (20 miles) beyond Bowness. North of the Wall, at its western end, lay three outpost forts, probably built, or at least planned, at this time. They may have been for early warning, but equally possibly protected those Brigantes left isolated by the construction of the Wall (see **90**).

This scheme was never completed. During construction, work appears to have halted while the soldier-builders turned to another

42 *Hadrian's Wall crossing Cuddy's Crag at Housesteads looking east.*

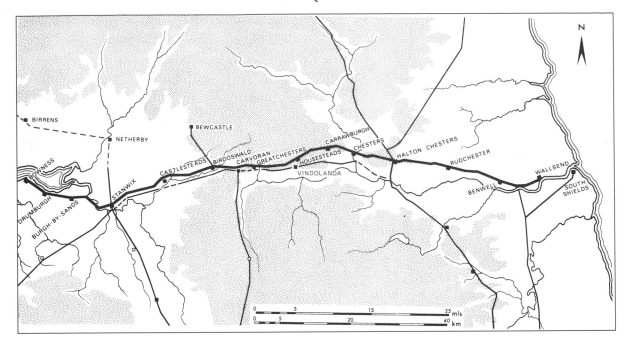

43 *Map of Hadrian's Wall as completed.*

task, the building of forts on the Wall (**43**). In the first scheme, the regiments had been left in their forts on the Stanegate behind the Wall. In the second plan, several of these forts were retained but new regiments were transferred from elsewhere in northern England and Wales and located in newly constructed forts which were actually placed astride the Wall itself. This was clearly a major task and there must have been a particular reason for the change. It seems probable that it was related to mobility. The Wall will have restricted the freedom of movement of the regiments in the forts to its rear and in order to provide them with greater mobility their new bases were built athwart the Wall. Now, instead of units having to negotiate movement through a single milecastle gateway in order to move north of the Wall, they had the equivalent of six such gateways for access to the Wall forts. Manoeuvrability to the south was aided by the addition of single portal side gates at each fort, a unique feature.

The construction of sixteen new forts must have considerably lengthened the building programme. It may be for this reason that when the soldiers resumed the construction of the Wall, its thickness was reduced from 10ft (3m) to somewhere between 6 and 8ft (2–2.5m). The advantage of this for us today is that the points where the stone wall was reduced in thickness survive and help us unravel the complexities of the building programme.

It was probably very shortly after the decision to add the forts to the Wall and while they were still being built that another decision was taken: to add an earthwork behind the Wall (**44**). This structure, known as the Vallum for well over 1000 years, since the time of the Venerable Bede, consisted of a central ditch with a mound set back on each side, the whole measuring 30m (100ft) across. It seems probable that this earthwork acted rather like the Roman equivalent of barbed wire. In other words, it was a clear southern boundary to the military zone.

The construction of the Vallum had a significant effect on how the Wall functioned. Previously, travellers had been able to choose from about 76 gates where they might cross the Wall. As crossing points over the Vallum ditch were only provided at forts, the number of access points was reduced to about 16. The reason for this is not known, but may reflect a desire to enable the senior officers at the forts to monitor the crossing points.

This was not the end of modifications to the Wall. It was extended 6.5km (4 miles) downstream from Newcastle to Wallsend, where another fort was built. A rather long gap between the forts at Chesters and Housesteads was plugged by a new fort at Carrawburgh. Interestingly, this fort was not built astride the Wall, but completely to the south, though still attached to it, as was Greatchesters, apparently built late in the sequence, and the remodelled Birdoswald. This, together with the blocking of some fort gateways at an early stage of their history, may imply that the army had realized that once the forts were on the Wall line it was not necessary for them to project to the north. Further west, a start was made on rebuilding the turf wall in stone, while at the very end of Hadrian's reign building was in progress at the fort at Carvoran.

The completed Wall was rather different from that planned. In the first scheme the two functions of frontier defence and frontier control had been separated: frontier defence rested with the regiments in the forts behind the Wall on the Stanegate and elsewhere, while frontier control was undertaken by the soldiers in the milecastles and turrets. In the second scheme, both functions were focused on the Wall itself. Thus Hadrian's Wall had developed while under construction. If its planner had seen how it would finish, he might have produced a different blueprint at the beginning. The construction of the Antonine Wall allowed a new frontier to be built integrating all the lessons learned during the construction of Hadrian's Wall.

The Antonine Wall

The Romans seem to have continued to modify Hadrian's Wall right up to the death of Hadrian in July 138. Within months of his death, however, it was abandoned in favour of a move north and the construction of a new Wall, in the words of the biographer of Antoninus Pius, 'this time of turf'.

44 *The central sector of Hadrian's Wall looking east. The Wall runs along the top of the crags with the Vallum occupying the low-lying ground to the right.*

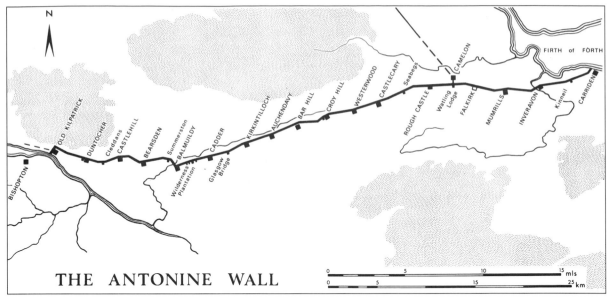

THE ANTONINE WALL

45 *Map of the Antonine Wall showing the known forts and fortlets. The original plan probably entailed fortlets at mile (1.6km) intervals, but not all are known.*

When Hadrian's Wall was planned there was already in existence a road across the Tyne–Solway isthmus linking the front-line forts and that, it appears, helped to determine the location of the Wall. No such road or line of forts helped determine the position of the Antonine Wall. This Wall was built on new ground and its hinterland forts were also all built *de novo*. Thus the Antonine Wall allows us to judge Roman planning uncluttered by previous developments.

The line chosen for the Antonine Wall was the Forth–Clyde isthmus (**45**). For much of its length it utilized the high ground along the southern edge of the central valley of Scotland. This valley is formed by the River Carron, flowing eastward into the Forth, and the River Kelvin, a tributary of the Clyde, in the west. Together, these rivers helped create a boggy foreground to the Wall before the land rose up to the Campsie Fells to the north. To the east, the Wall simply ran down the slope to terminate on the edge of the Forth. At the west end there was a different problem. The aim of the builders appears to have been to end the Wall on the

north side of the Clyde as far downstream as to control as many fording points as possible. Thus at Balmuildy, where the Kelvin turned sharply southwards, the Wall left its convenient topographical line and thereafter zigzagged across country from high point to high point until it reached the Clyde at Old Kilpatrick.

The details of the line of the Wall are interesting too. Across Croy Hill it took the straightest route and did not deviate to follow the crest of the ridge (**46**). Thus, 'dead ground' was left in front of the Wall. For its western 3km (2 miles) the Wall ran along a reverse slope so that the lie of the land was against the Romans. These two examples are among the factors which suggest that the primary purpose of the Antonine Wall was not military.

The Antonine Wall was built of turf (**colour plate 7**). The 'wall' itself was a turf rampart, probably intended to be 15 Roman feet (4.5m) wide, placed on a stone base. During the Glasgow Archaeology Society's excavations in the 1890s some early experimental archaeology was undertaken. All the fallen turves were placed on top of the surviving rampart at Rough Castle and this demonstrated that the rampart would have been at least 3m (10ft) high. It is possible that it was surmounted by a timber breastwork (**47**).

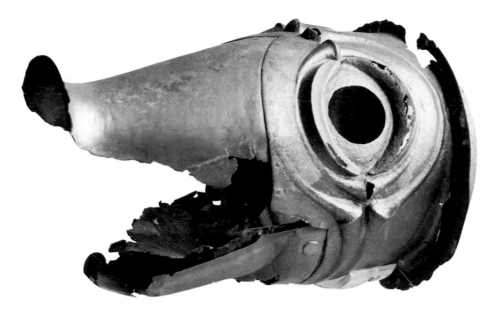

1 *This boar's head formed part of a war trumpet found at Deskford in Aberdeenshire; it may have been used by a Caledonian army.*

2 *The head of Constantine the Great, in Rome. The very size of the head emphasizes the nature of the Roman empire: a military dictatorship.*

3 *A legionary soldier of the early second century carrying his kit (drawn by Peter Connolly).*

4 *An auxiliary cavalryman (left) and infantryman of the early second century (drawn by Peter Connolly).*

5 *The Roman road, Dere Street, crossing Soutra Hill south of Edinburgh. To the near side of the road platform a quarry pit is visible.*

6 *Durisdeer fortlet and the southern approaches of the Dalveen pass looking south.*

7 A section through the rampart of the Antonine Wall at Tentfield Plantation, cut by Professor Anne Robertson in 1965.

8 The fort at Rough Castle on the Antonine Wall looking east. The fort lies to the right of the Antonine Wall, whose ditch is clearly visible; the annexe is attached to the far side of the fort.

9 The bath-house at Bearsden looking south. The main spine of the building runs from the changing-room to the right through the cold room and three rooms of the steam range to the furnace. To this side of the cold room is the hot dry room and beyond the cold bath. Top left lies the latrine.

10 An artist's impression of the communal latrine in the fort annexe at Bearsden (drawn by Michael J. Moore).

11 *The Falkirk hoard, dating to about 230, contained about 2000 silver denarii.*

12 *This group of bowls, mostly of bronze and dating to the later second century and later, was found at Helmsdale in Sutherland. The bowls may have reached northern Scotland through trade, or perhaps as a diplomatic gift.*

13 *Traprain Law from the north. Quarrying has now ceased at the site*

14 *Some of the objects in the Traprain Treasure dating to about 400.*

15 *Within the ramparts of the fort at Edin's Hall sits a broch probably dating to the second century* AD. *An open settlement overlies the hill-fort defences at the top of the picture.*

16 *A settlement of four stone houses and a souterrain at Ardestie near Dundee. The souterrain, an underground passage, is generally considered to have been used for storage.*

46 *The Antonine Wall crossing Croy Hill look-*
ing east. 'Dead' ground lies to the left (north) of
the Wall at the top of the photograph.

47 *An artist's impression of the building of the*
Antonine Wall. This illustrates several activities
which would not have taken place at the same
time: the laying of the stone base, the placing of
the turf blocks, cut to regulation size 18 by 12 by
6in, and the construction of the breastwork.
Drawn by Michael J. Moore.

48 *The Antonine Wall ditch at Watling Lodge looking west to the site of the fortlet. This is the best surviving stretch of ditch.*

The rampart was, in fact, not always of turf. For the eastern 10km (6 miles) it was built of clay, or of earth revetted by clay blocks. There is also a hint that the original intention was to construct the wall of stone, for the fort at Balmuildy, one of the earliest structures to be built on the Wall, was provided with stone wing walls as if its builders were anticipating that the whole wall was to be of stone.

In front of the rampart lay a wide and deep ditch (48), the material from which was tipped out to the north to form a wide, low mound, commonly known as the upcast or outer mound. The turf from under this mound was not always used in the construction of the rampart. Recent excavations at three points have led to the discovery of small pits on the berm between the rampart and the ditch. These, like those located at Rough Castle in 1903, may have been an extra defence.

There was one other linear feature which appears to have been primary – a road, the Military Way. This lay a little distance behind the rampart. No road seems to have been constructed along Hadrian's Wall during Hadrian's reign: perhaps the Stanegate was considered sufficient together with the path which appears to have lain on the north berm of the Vallum. The lack of an existing road across the Forth–Clyde isthmus will have rendered the construction of one an obvious necessity.

Unlike on Hadrian's Wall, it was planned from the first that there would be forts on the Antonine Wall. The evidence for this has come through excavation. The forts at Mumrills, Castlecary and Balmuildy were all built before the rampart, while Old Kilpatrick was contemporary with the rampart: we believe that the Wall was built from east to west, so this would explain the difference at Old Kilpatrick. Balmuildy has produced two building inscriptions naming Lollius Urbicus, the governor responsible for the successful invasion of southern Scotland in 140. No governor is named on the building stones from the Wall itself, so perhaps Urbicus commenced building, leaving his unnamed successor to complete it.

No forts were placed astride the wall; all were built behind the rampart like the later forts on Hadrian's Wall. Yet there is a difference between the forts on the two Walls. On Hadrian's Wall the forts followed their own plan and gave the appearance of only incidentally being part of the frontier. On the Antonine Wall, however, the forts related very closely to the rampart, clearly respecting its existence.

Several of the forts had annexes, enclosures only slightly less defended than the forts themselves. Interestingly there is no Vallum on the Antonine Wall, just as there are no annexes beside the forts on Hadrian's Wall, though they are known in connection with earlier forts. As we believe that the Vallum shielded the rear of the military zone, it seems likely that the annexes were military in purpose, with the civilians living beyond both fort and annexe.

The original proposal appears to have been for six forts, about 13km (8 miles) apart. Each fort was large enough to hold a complete auxiliary regiment, though Castlecary always seems to have held a detachment. Between the forts were fortlets, similar in size to the milecastles on Hadrian's Wall and perhaps serving a similar function. Yet if one purpose was to provide access across the frontier, there is a problem, for none of the fortlets appears to have been provided with a causeway across the ditch in front of the gate. There is precisely the same problem on Hadrian's Wall. It is possible to argue that bridges were provided, but none has been found.

No towers have yet been discovered on the Antonine Wall, but other small structures are known. It has long been appreciated that at six points there is a southern expansion to the rampart. These expansions survive in pairs. Excavation has revealed a stone base against the rear of the rampart on which had been constructed a turf platform. At one, traces of

burning lay beside the platform, together with some fragments of Roman pottery. It was suggested that fires had been lit on top of the expansion, and that the expansions worked in pairs to send signals north and south of the Wall (49). This theory is plausible on topographical grounds, for the four eastern expansions do look northwards over open country while the western two look south up Clydesdale. It is also possible, though, that the burning was caused by fires lit by soldiers in hearths on the ground while they were at the site undertaking some other kind of activity.

Recently the situation has been complicated by the discovery of what appears to have been a seventh expansion. Excavation at Inveravon revealed the side of a platform built against the back of the rampart. Although only one side, and a corner, were located, the remains are very similar to those of the known expansions. However, the platform sits on low ground and is not in an obvious signalling position.

A second type of small structure was also identified recently on the Antonine Wall. On either side of the fortlet at Wilderness Plantation, Gordon Maxwell recognized the outline of three small enclosures. The four sites – fortlet and enclosures – are very roughly one-sixth of a Roman mile (0.25km) apart. Subsequent excavation established that one was primary, measuring about 5.5m (18ft) square within a rampart and ditch. No evidence was found of any structure within the rampart, so the enclosure's function remains uncertain.

We thus have on the Antonine Wall not only two series of structures of uncertain purpose, but an indication that more remain to be found.

Modifications to the Antonine Wall

Before the Wall was completed considerable modifications were set in hand, just as on Hadrian's Wall. The main change was the addition of about ten new forts to the Wall: some are known to have been placed beside existing

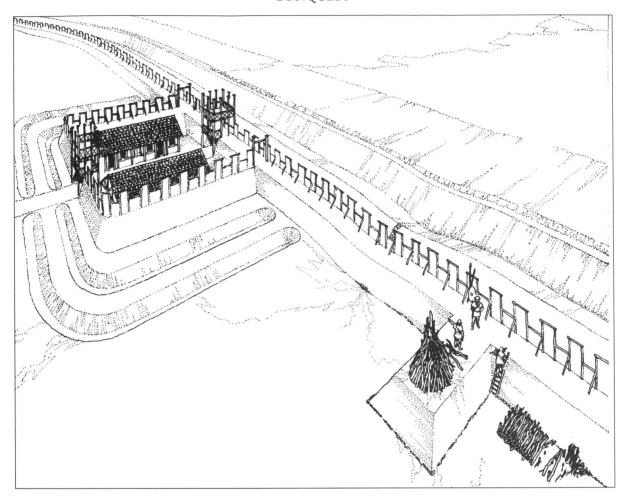

49 *An artist's impression of the Antonine Wall showing an expansion in the foreground, restored as a beacon platform, and a fortlet beyond. Drawn by Michael J. Moore.*

fortlets. There seems to have been a difference in the treatment of the western and eastern sectors of the Wall. In the eastern half, few secondary forts are known, and those which do exist are all relatively small (**colour plate 8**), certainly smaller than those in the western half where each secondary fort was capable of holding a complete regiment. It is possible that the existence of outpost forts beyond the eastern end of the Wall was considered sufficient in itself, rendering the construction of new forts in this sector unnecessary.

The building of the Antonine Wall

The Antonine Wall was built by the Roman army. Inscriptions survive indicating that both legionaries and auxiliaries built, or rebuilt, the forts on the Wall. Among these inscriptions, however, are twenty highly ornamented slabs recording the erection of the frontier, the *opus valli*, the work of the Wall (**50** and see **15, 31**). These stones record the distances constructed by each of the three legions of the province, *II Augusta, VI Victrix* and *XX Valeria Victrix*, and are termed 'distance-slabs'. They reveal that the 40 Roman mile-long Wall (60km) was divided into sectors, with each of the three legions apparently building equal lengths (1 Roman mile=4860ft=1481m). Most of the Wall was measured in paces in lengths of 4²/₃,

50 *The Hutcheson Hill distance-slab. In the centre a laurel wreath is placed in the beak of the eagle of* legio XX Valeria Victrix *watched by bound captives.*

$3^{2}/_{3}$ and 3 Roman miles. The western 6.5km (4 miles), however, were measured in feet. The reason for this is not known, but it is interesting that the change in the unit of measurement occurred around the point the original builders had reached when it was decided to add forts to the Wall, and it is possible that these two factors are related. It has recently been suggested that the original plan had included the construction of a Vallum, but this was abandoned before work had commenced to be replaced by annexes at individual forts.

While the legions were in the north building the Wall, they lived in temporary camps. Several of these have been located along the Wall. At each end of the eastern $4^{2}/_{3}$ stretch built by *II Augusta*, two camps have been discovered, and a further two lie at the eastern end of the next sector to the west. Thus it appears that groups of soldiers might have started working towards each other from both ends of their stretch at the same time, with the groups possibly divided into rampart and ditch gangs.

The purpose of the Antonine Wall

The placing of forts on Hadrian's Wall during its construction and the continuation of that pattern on the Antonine Wall obscured the operation of two different functions undertaken by the army: defence and frontier control. The purpose of the regiments on the Antonine Wall – and those in front and behind, linked to the Wall by roads (**51** and see **colour plate 5**)) – was to protect the province from attack as well as help police the neighbouring provincials. The Wall, however, was erected in order to aid frontier control. A linear barrier, such as Hadrian's Wall and the Antonine Wall, was the most effective way of controlling the movement of people. Thus the walls were bureaucratic in concept, not military. This is not to say that they served no military purpose: they would certainly have slowed down an invasion of the province, but they would no more have stopped it than the Berlin Wall would have halted a major invasion.

The Antonine Wall, like Hadrian's Wall, divided the 'barbarians' from the Romans. It allowed the province to develop peacefully to the rear, and it is to the province and its life that we will now turn.

51 *The Ingliston milestone, erected in the reign of Antoninus Pius, on one of the roads linking the Antonine Wall with the province to the south.*

CHAPTER FOUR

Occupation

The framework of the Roman occupation was based on the fort. Our view of a Roman fort is coloured by establishments such as Housesteads where the surviving stone walls give the impression of solid permanence. The fort, however, had grown out of the temporary camp and winter-quarters. While the camp only contained tents, the accommodation in winter-quarters would have been more substantial. Caesar's army constructed huts with thatched roofs in Gaul. Early forts in Scotland may have been rather similar. Certainly they were often a lot more temporary than forts such as Housesteads.

In the early years of the conquest the army was still feeling its way and it was prepared to move forts until the most suitable location, and size of force, was determined. Thus at Dalswinton in Nithsdale there are two adjacent forts, each with two main periods. The first, and larger, fort was on the flood plain and probably abandoned for that reason. After remodelling, it was succeeded by a smaller, but still substantial, fort on the higher ground overlooking the river. This fort contained timber buildings: the nature of the structures in the earlier forts is unknown. All this activity appears to have taken place in the decade following Agricola's arrival in 79.

The Roman fort

The fort provided accommodation for a group of soldiers. The usual group was a regiment of 500 or 1000 men, infantry, cavalry or mixed.

There was a certain pattern to the arrangement of the buildings within a fort, but it was not too inflexible (52). The normal plan was for the headquarters building (*principia*) to sit in the centre, flanked to the right by a large house for the commanding officer (*praetorium*) and to the left by one or more granaries (*horreum*). In front and behind this central range of buildings lay barrack blocks, stables and storehouses. The latrine was normally beside the rampart allowing the sewage to drain out of the fort. Some forts contained a hospital, usually placed in the central range. All were surrounded by a rampart of turf and two or more ditches, broken by gates, normally four, which opened on to roads leading across the fort (53).

Certain communal facilities, such as mess rooms and canteens, were not provided. The only general-purpose room was a central assembly hall situated in the headquarters building (see 58). At the front of this building lay a courtyard, normally surrounded by a covered veranda. Although the courtyard contained a well, often the only one in the fort, its function otherwise is not clear. Possibly notices, such as the orders for the day and the duty rotas, were displayed on the verandas. Through the courtyard lay the assembly hall (*basilica*). At the right-hand end was a platform or tribunal, presumably for the use of the commanding officer. At the rear of the headquarters building lay five rooms. The central one was the regimental shrine (*aedes*), containing an

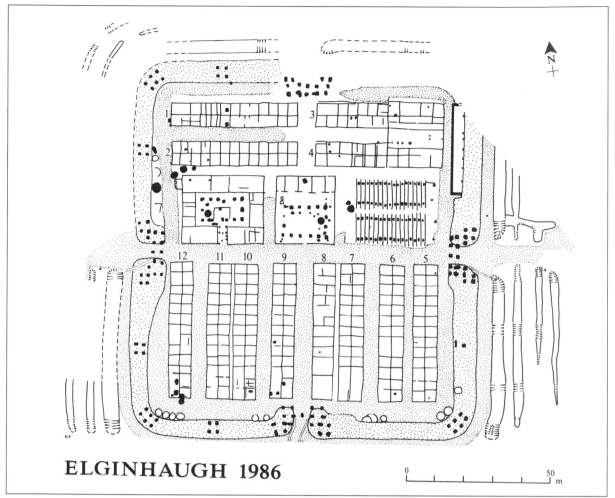

ELGINHAUGH 1986

0   50
m

*52 Plan of the fort at Elginhaugh. The head-
quarters building in the centre is flanked, left, by
the commander's house and, right, by two granaries. To north and south lie barrack blocks.*

*53 The army stands in front of a fort gate.
Towers project above the ramparts. The building
inside the fort appears to be a granary.*

altar and statue of the emperor, probably
flanked by the unit's standards: usually the regimental treasure chest was kept here. This may
have been because there was a guard on duty at
the shrine. The other rooms were offices for the
clerks and accountants of the unit.

The accommodation reflected the hierarchy
within the regiment. The commanding officer
had his own house which he shared with his
wife, family and slaves. At the end of each

54 *A 'cut-away' of the bath-house at Bar Hill on the Antonine Wall, with the heated rooms to the right and the cold room, changing-room and latrine to the left. Drawn by Michael J. Moore.*

55 *An artist's impression of the fort at Bar Hill on the Antonine Wall. To the left of the headquarters building is the commander's house, to the right a granary and two other buildings; to north and south lie barrack blocks. The bath-house is placed in the top corner of the fort. Drawn by Michael J. Moore.*

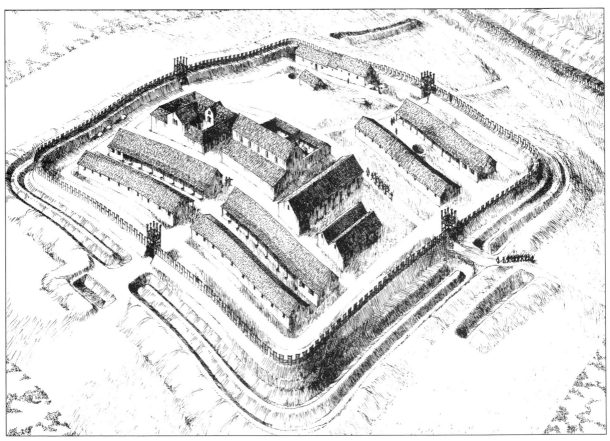

barrack block lay accommodation for the centurion or decurion. This consisted of a suite of rooms, and might include a latrine. The centurion was allowed to marry and his wife may have lived with him: an inscription found at Westerwood on the Antonine Wall records the wife and family of a legionary centurion. The soldiers, on the other hand, were arranged eight to a room. They were not allowed to marry. Many, however, had relationships with the women who lived in the civil settlements outside the forts and these common law marriages were recognized retrospectively by the army when the soldiers retired.

Another group of men who lived in the fort were the slaves. Officers and soldiers owned slaves either individually or in groups. We know nothing about their living arrangements.

The care of the Roman army for the health and hygiene of its troops is reflected not only by the hospital but by the provision of a communal latrine and a bath-house, usually containing its own latrine, at each fort (**54, 55, colour plates 9** and **10**). The bath-house was provided for the use of all soldiers in the fort, though we do not know how often they bathed. In the bath-house soldiers were offered a choice of bathing – the steam or Turkish bath (inherited by the Turks from the Romans) and the hot dry or sauna treatment. The bath-house might be inside the fort, though often it was built in an adjacent annexe. The annexe was also the location of small-scale industrial activities, though so little excavation has been undertaken within them that our knowledge is very slight. Beyond both fort and annexe lay the regimental parade ground.

Forts, fortresses and fortlets

While we believe that many forts were built for single units, others were clearly not. Second-century Newstead appears to have held a cavalry regiment and a legionary detachment. Other forts held less than a complete unit. Birrens, in the second century, does not appear

to have contained a full complement of buildings for the regiment attested as being stationed there: presumably no accommodation was provided for the soldiers outstationed in the neighbouring fortlets.

The legionary fortress was, in some ways, an auxiliary fort writ large, but it was more than than. It contained a headquarters building, a large house for the legate and several smaller houses for the other senior officers, a hospital, workshop, barrack blocks, granaries and storerooms (see **39**). The sheer size of the fortress at 20ha (50 acres) and the number of men based there – about 5000 – in effect meant that this was a small town. The regular layout facilitated the soldiers undertaking their duties within its confines.

Officers and men

A common phrase today acknowledges the distinction between officers and men. In the Roman army there were senior officers, officers and men (**56**). At the top of a regimental

56 *Officers and standard bearers on Trajan's Column.*

hierarchy was the commanding officer, a member of the lower aristocracy or gentry. His nearest equivalent in social status was the commanding officer of the neighbouring auxiliary unit. The prefect or tribune – the exact title depended upon the rank of the unit – normally held his post for three years and thereafter may have continued up the hierarchy or, if he was judged of insufficient standard, not given another appointment.

The backbone of each unit were the centurions and decurions. They were long-serving officers, who had no fixed term of appointment and, it would appear, could literally continue in service until they dropped: the longest-serving centurion had sixty-one years with the colours. Most centurions and decurions had risen through the ranks, though it was possible to enter by means of a direct commission.

The bulk of the unit, of course, consisted of the ordinary soldiers. Most were recruited between the ages of 18 and 21 and enlisted for twenty-five years. The life expectancy of soldiers was better than civilians of similar age and roughly half would survive to receive Roman citizenship, the reward for service in the army: the legionaries already citizens, in comparison, received a lump sum on retirement. The Roman army primarily relied upon local recruitment, often recruiting the sons of soldiers from the settlements outside forts. Accordingly, most soldiers serving on the northern frontier would be recruited from Britain, though some came from Gaul and Germany. One soldier who died at the fort at Mumrills on the Antonine Wall was a Brigantian from northern England (57). When *cohors II Tungrorum* was temporarily stationed in modern southern Germany it recruited local men, who returned with the regiment to Britain, to erect altars to their strange-sounding German gods at Birrens.

Soldiers were not, however, all the same rank or status. Some were *immunes*, soldiers rendered immune from general fatigues in return for carrying out other duties. Among

57 *The tombstone of Nectovelius, a Brigantian, soldier in the Third Cohort of Thracians, who died after nine years' service and was buried at Mumrills on the Antonine Wall.*

the *immunes* were surveyors, architects, medical orderlies, carpenters, glaziers, armourers, musicians, clerks and accountants. Perhaps as many as 20 per cent of the soldiers in any regiment were either *immunes* or promoted.

Several posts carried extra rank and pay. Each century had a second-in-command known as the *optio*, because the centurion had originally exercised his choice or option in selecting the soldier; a third-in-command, the *tesserarius*, so called because he formerly carried the *tessera* or tile bearing the password; and a standard bearer, the *signifer*, who also served as the century's accounts officer. There were other promoted posts including the *cornicularius*, the adjutant in charge of the regimental office, and the *custos armorum*, who looked after each century's weapons. Some of these posts were graded *sesquiplicarii*, that is their holder received pay-and-a-half, and others *duplicarii*, double-pay posts. Cavalry were paid more than infantry, so there was probably quite a variety of pay grades.

A soldier could rise through these posts to centurion or decurion. He would first have to become an *immunis*, after at least three years' service normally. Thereafter he would seek a post as a *sesquiplicarius*, such as *custos armorum* or *tesserarius*, before becoming eligible for *optio, signifer* or *cornicularius*. If the soldier aspired to the centurionate he would have to gain experience of administration (say *cornicularius* or *signifer*) as well as command (*optio*).

Life in the fort

The Roman army was a highly organized institution. Its members across the whole empire broadly followed the same daily, and annual, routine. The day commenced with the morning report. On 27 May 239, for example, the senior centurion of *cohors XX Palmyrenorum* based at Dura Europos on the Euphrates gave the morning report. This firstly recorded the number of officers and men in the unit, arranged by rank and type. There followed the password for the day, Security, and the names of the soldiers standing watch at the standards. Other reports list the men leaving and returning to the base that day.

Sentry duty was one important task. Other soldiers undertook fatigues such as cleaning officers' uniforms, cleaning the streets, bath-house tasks, or, outside the fort, building roads – or frontiers. It was possible to escape such fatigues by obtaining an appointment as a clerk or on a senior officer's staff. The normal procedure in the Roman world was simply to ask for an appointment. In 107 Julius Apollinaris went to see Claudius Severus, governor of Arabia, and sought a position on his staff. He was advised that there was no vacancy in that office, but the governor was also legionary legate and he did have a post available on that staff. Accordingly Apollinaris was advised to report to the adjutant in charge of the legate's staff. He wrote home to tell his father that he was not suffering the fate of his comrades who where cutting building stone all day.

Julius Apollinaris would have worked in the equivalent of one of the rooms at the rear of the headquarters building (58). Here were prepared the files and reports which were an integral part of army life. The Roman army was so bureaucratic that receipts were issued in quadruplicate! Each soldier had his own file which recorded all details about his recruitment and career: there

58 *An artist's impression of the headquarters building at Bar Hill. The clerks worked in the rooms at the back. Drawn by Michael J. Moore.*

were even files on army horses. Duty rotas were prepared and careful records were kept of the whereabouts of each soldier. A return was made annually by each unit listing the number of officers and soldiers, the accessions and losses, the location of all soldiers in the regiment, and the balance. There were orders for equipment and receipts, letters and accounts.

Several of these documents are represented in the Vindolanda archive. They include a strength report of the First Cohort of Tungrians dated 18 May probably within the period 92 to 97. This records that 456 soldiers were absent, 46 serving in the guard of the governor in London and 337 at Coria (presumably Corbridge); 15 soldiers were sick, 6 wounded and 10 suffered from inflammation of the eyes (see 60), leaving only 265 of the unit strength of 752 available for active service at the parent fort, Vindolanda. Another writing tablet lists the location of soldiers on a 25 April: 343 in the workshops, including 12 shoemakers and 18 at the bath-house; the document also mentions lead, wagons, the hospital, kilns, clay and plasterers.

There are also many lists and accounts. An unusual document is a list headed 'Revenues of the fort' and includes different sums of money for 27 to 31 July, totalling 80+ *denarii*. Another is a cash account of sums received and debts outstanding by individuals. One list includes references to blankets, loose robes, vests, tunics and a *paenula*, an Italian cape which was an item of military equipment; another an overcoat and a towel. A further list includes a coverlet and a bedspread; another a shallow dish, side plates, vinegar bowls, eggcups, a platter, a bronze lamp, bread-baskets, cups and a bowl. Many documents are records of payments of many kinds, for food, a horse, tallow, iron, timber, a towel, clothing and shoes.

Vindolanda has produced a new type of report, a check, perhaps made daily, on personnel and equipment. That for a particular 13 March can be restored as: 'Report of the ninth Cohort of Batavians. All who ought to be at

their posts are there, and they will see to the baggage, which is present, Candidus, *optio* [second-in-command to the centurion] of the century of Felicio, submitted the report.'

The sheer amount of 'paperwork' which a unit must have accumulated during a sojourn of twenty years on the Antonine Wall would have been enormous. We know so much about *cohors XX Palmyrenorum* stationed at Dura Europos on the Euphrates because when the fort was attacked in 256 part of the archive, stretching back over nearly fifty years, was used to help heighten the city's ramparts.

The commanding officer

The Vindolanda writing tablets also include several separate correspondence archives of the commanding officers which illustrate their work and relaxation. The letters include references to transactions and supplies; one records the approval of clothing and a request for cloaks and tunics; another, from a woman, requests a favour. There is also a letter to the commanding officer asking him to recommend a third person to the centurion at Carlisle. In one letter Hostilius Flavianus wrote offering Cerealis a fortunate and happy New Year...!

Several letters are between different commanding officers. One of the most remarkable is to the wife of the prefect at Vindolanda from the wife of one of his colleagues:

Claudia Severa to her Lepidina greetings. On 11 September, sister, for the day of the celebrations on my birthday, I give you a warm invitation to make sure that you come to us, to make the day more enjoyable for me by your arrival, if you are present[?]. Give my greeting to your Cerealis. My Aelius and my little son send him[?] their greetings.

The letter ends with a note by Severa herself: 'I shall expect you, sister. Farewell, sister, my dearest soul, as I hope to prosper, and hail'.

A second letter states that Claudia Severa had obtained her husband's permission to visit

Lepidina whenever she wished. A further letter to Lepidina, this time from Paterna, reveals another aspect of life on the northern frontier. The writer informs Lepidina that she is bringing 'two remedies[?], the one for..., the other for fever[?]' (**59, 60**).

The letters underline the social isolation of the commanding officer, his wife and family. Claudia Severa and Lepidina had no social equals within their own forts. Indeed, while subtleties of rank and degree separated the commanding officers into a distinct pecking order, none was in charge of another. In fact the nearest senior officer was the legionary legate in York, and beyond him the governor in London. The fort at Newstead was the largest in Scotland in the second century, but that does not indicate that the commanding officer there had any authority over his colleagues in day-to-day operations. Presumably each regiment looked after its own territory. Perhaps, when necessary, units combined with the senior of the commanding officers taking charge of the force, but we can only surmise, we do not know how command and cooperation worked on the frontier.

Food

The Roman soldier had a varied diet. Wheat was the staple item and was used to make bread, porridge and pasta (**61**). Barley was used in broth; it was also used as punishment rations for the men. Analysis of the sewage at Bearsden on the Antonine Wall has demonstrated that the diet was mainly vegetarian but both literary sources and archaeology demonstrate that meat was also eaten. Cattle, sheep and pig were the most popular, in that order, but deer, hare and other wild animals, fowl, fish and shellfish were also eaten. Fruit included apples, pears, plums, cherries,

59 *This fragment of pottery, probably from a wine jar, bears an inscription in Greek recording that it once contained wine flavoured with horehound, a cough medicine.*

60 *A stamp for sealing a container of eye ointment: found at Tranent, East Lothian. The inscription reads, in reverse:* L VALLATINI APALOCROCODES AD DIATHESIS, *(Lucius Vallatinus' mild* crocodes *for the eyes).*

61 *Querns and cooking pots found at Newstead.*

62 *Jars (amphorae) used for transporting wine, olives and similar items.*

peaches, grapes, elderberries, damsons, apricots, blackberries, strawberries, raspberries, olives, pomegranates, cloves and figs. In addition there were nuts: sweet chestnuts, hazelnuts, walnuts and beechnuts. The wide range of vegetables included lentils, cabbage, peas, broad beans and horsebeans, carrots, rice and celery. Cheese and eggs should not be forgotten, nor salt and vinegar. Wine, sour wine (mixed with water to make *posca*) and Celtic beer are mentioned on several writing tablets at Vindolanda (**62**).

The Vindolanda writing tablets include many references to food: wheat, barley, bread, twisted loaves(?), pork, ham, bacon, bacon-lard, pork-fat, roe-deer, venison, chickens, beans(?), lentils, lovage, radishes, olives, meal, fish-sauce, oysters, gruel, apples, butter(?), eggs, honey, oil, pepper and spices. There are also references to the ox herds at the wood, Candidus in charge of the pigs, and the brewer.

Even on the Antonine Wall, the north-west frontier of the Roman empire, a wide variety of foods was available. The sewage at Bearsden contained fragments of wheat, barley, bean, fig, dill, coriander, opium poppy (possibly used on

bread as today), hazelnut, raspberry, bramble, wild strawberry, bilberry and celery. Fig, dill, coriander and celery, the seeds of which were used as spices and medicinally, may have been imported from the Mediterranean. Linseed was used in poultices; the pollen of mallow suggests that mallow flowers were eaten for their medicinal properties. The soldiers suffered from whipworm and roundworm, and some of their grain appear to have been contaminated with weevils.

Normally two meals were eaten each day, what we would call breakfast and supper. An Egyptian papyrus of 360 records a ration of 3lb of bread, 2lb of meat, 2 pints of wine and $\frac{1}{8}$ pint of oil per soldier per day. In theory at least, each soldier was provided with a daily ration of food which he cooked himself. The Carvoran measure from Hadrian's Wall, however, holds the equivalent of seven daily rations and suggests that the grain was disbursed weekly.

Hearths and ovens were frequently placed on the open space immediately inside the rampart. But whether soldiers used them on an individual basis is unknown. As soldiers slept eight or ten to a room, it seems likely that they pooled their food with one man taking on the cooking for the group, a normal occurrence with any such body. This is supported by the discovery of cooking implements marked with the name of barrack-room groups (*contubernia*).

A study of mortality in the Roman empire has suggested that, up to retirement, soldiers, despite their profession, had a greater life expectancy than civilians: then the position was reversed and civilians fared better. The food and medical care given to soldiers and their active lives must have played a large part in securing their welfare.

Training

Training was an important part of army life. Each recruit received basic training in arms and weapons, drill and movements, running and jumping, military discipline and camp building. This training continued throughout

63 *These face masks from Newstead would have been worn during military exercises.*

his career, and was supplemented by marching at military and rapid paces, swimming, vaulting over wooden horses, tree felling and cross-country route-marches of 32km (20 miles) three times a month.

The parade ground was the scene of much training. None has been located in Scotland, but some are known outside forts in northern England. A large area was levelled and metalled. This was used for basic training and also for exercises when the soldiers wore special uniforms, including face masks (**63**). Exercises included mock battles between Greeks and Amazons. The Emperor Hadrian inspected such exercises in Africa during his visit there in 128 and it is possible that he witnessed similar events in Britain when he was here in 122.

Legionary fortresses were generally provided with amphitheatres, perhaps used for training as well as shows. One possible amphitheatre has recently been recognized outside the fort at Newstead.

Not all training took place at the fort. In south-west Scotland there is a site which appears to have been a training area for the army of the northern frontier. A camp lay on each side of the prehistoric hill-fort at Burnswark; one contained semi-permanent structures (**64**). On top of the abandoned entrances to the hill-fort Roman

64 *On each side of Burnswark Hill lies a Roman camp. Each of the three mounds in front of the entrances in the south camp faced a target laid out over the abandoned gates of the prehistoric fort on top of the hill.*

65 *Ballista balls and sling bullets found at Burnswark. Lead sling bullets have been found at Birrens, Housesteads, Birdoswald, Vindolanda, Corbridge and Ambleside, possibly indicating the range of units which used the training area.*

66 *A slinger depicted on Trajan's Column.*

gates were laid out in plan using flagstones. These were targets for stone shot fired by catapults placed on mounds in front of the camp gates. The sling bullets found at Burnswark were made of lead, though such bullets were normally of clay (**65, 66**).

Pay

Soldiers were paid three times a year. The first payment took place at the time of the annual New Year parade. While we know that in the second century legionaries were paid 300 *denarii* a year, the amount paid to auxiliary soldiers is uncertain. As in most armies, cavalry were paid more than infantry.

The pay was placed in the soldier's bank account which was administered by his standard bearer. Pay records survive written in the different hands of successive standard bearers (see **56**). Deductions were made for hay, food, boots and socks, clothing and the camp Saturnalia dinner (25 December). Receipts for food received by soldiers are known. In addition, each soldier had to pay for his own arms and armour and a share of his tent: presumably on enlistment and further charges only made when necessary thereafter. These items were purchased back by the army from the soldier or his heir when he retired or died.

These were the official charges. Tacitus, in describing the mutiny which followed Augustus' death in AD 14, recorded that among the complaints of the soldiers was that they had to pay bribes to brutal centurions. They also had to pay centurions for leave, until the emperor took over this responsibility. Several writing tablets at Vindolanda are requests for leave: 'I, Messicus..., ask, my lord, that you consider me a worthy person to whom to grant leave at Coria [probably Corbridge].'

Religion

A fragmentary document, dating to about 225, found at Dura Europos on the Euphrates lists

67 *Each year every regiment in the army renewed its vows to Jupiter, chief deity in the Roman pantheon, for the well-being of the Roman emperor and the Roman State. This dedication to Jupiter was made by L. Minthonius Tertullus, prefect of the the Fifth Cohort of Gauls stationed at Cramond.*

68 *A statue of Mars found in the annexe of Balmuildy fort on the Antonine Wall.*

69 *The head of a goddess, probably Fortuna, found in the bath-house at Bearsden. Fortuna is often found in bath-houses where she protected men from the evil eye.*

official holy days which would be celebrated across the whole empire and includes festivals marking the accession and birthdays of past and present emperors and their wives. Forty-two festivals, and the appropriate sacrifice for the day, are listed. Two days were of particular importance: 3 January when, on behalf of himself and his unit, every commander renewed his vows to Jupiter for the well-being of the emperor and his empire, and the anniversary of the emperor's succession, when a similar ceremony took place (**67**).

Other gods in the Roman pantheon were worshipped: Juno, Mars (**68**), Mercury, Minerva, Diana, Neptune, Apollo and Hercules, as well as gods closely connected with the emperor such as Victory and Discipline (see **76**), or army life like the goddess of the parade ground. Fortuna, often

found in bath-houses, protected men from the evil eye (**69**). Foreign gods might be favoured by recruits from abroad, or perhaps worshipped by regiments remembering their place of foundation: Harimella, Ricagambeda and Viradecthis at

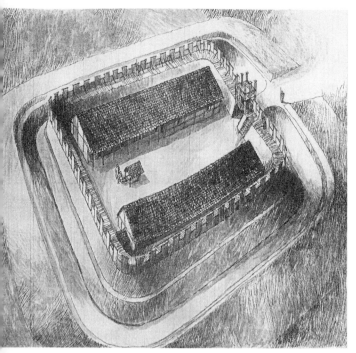

70 *An artist's impression of the fortlet at Barburgh Mill in south-west Scotland. Drawn by Michael J. Moore.*

Birrens. Nor were local gods such as Brigantia forgotten, who was also commemorated at Birrens (see **90**).

Official cults were represented by altars erected in the headquarters building, such as the altar to the Discipline of the Emperor discovered at Birrens. Other gods and goddesses might have their own temple or shrine, such as Mercury at Castlecary on the Antonine Wall (see **8**).

Temples and shrines may also have existed in the countryside. A stone platform found in the 1960s on a hill in the Tweed valley may have been the foundation of a rural temple, perhaps to Silvanus. The marble head found at Hawkshaw (see **34**) and the monumental leg from a bronze statue discovered at Milsington, both in the Borders, may also point to the existence of rural shrines.

The dedications can often tell us something about the dedicator himself. Four altars erected by M. Cocceius Firmus, centurion of *legio II Augusta*, at Auchendavy on the Antonine Wall included a wide range of gods:

Jupiter, Victorious Victory, Diana, Apollo, the *Genius* of the land of Britain, Mars, Minerva, the goddesses of the parade ground, Hercules, Epona and Victory. The combination of gods suggests that Firmus came from the lower Danube and had previously served in the emperor's guard in Rome. Cocceius Firmus may be the same as the centurion of that name who is recorded in the Digest of Roman Law as having his female slave stolen by bandits from the salt-mines where she was serving her prison sentence, subsequently buying her back.

Life outside the fort

The fort provided a permanent home for soldiers, but it was a base not a garrison-town. Thus soldiers would spend long periods away from their forts. Documents of *cohors XX Palmyrenorum* based at Dura Europos reveal that soldiers might be on outpost duty for three years and more. Presumably the soldiers stationed in the fortlets of south-west Scotland in the second century would be away from their parent units for such a period, or even longer (**70, 71**).

Training would, as we have seen, take soldiers away from their forts, but so would their two main functions: to maintain peace within

71 *A gaming board found at Bearsden fort. Such games would have helped soldiers while away their time on outpost duty.*

the province and defend it from attack. Thus, presumably, soldiers maintained surveillance over the tribesmen of the frontier zone, both within and without the province. Regular patrolling would have been undertaken and tribal meetings would only have taken place under military supervision. The army operated the regulations governing the movement of people into and out of the province. They not only escorted travellers in the frontier regions but also furnished escorts for convoys to ensure that they were not attacked by brigands.

The tribes living beyond the frontier would also have been subjected to Roman surveillance and interference. The Romans did not regard these tribes as independent sovereign States but considered that they had a right to interfere in the internal affairs of States beyond the frontier to ensure that peace was maintained. This is considered in more detail in Chapter 6.

Administration and government in the frontier zone

The Romans generally preferred to use the existing tribal leaders to govern on their behalf and each province was made up of a number of self-governing units. In Britain these local self-governing units were mostly based on the pre-Roman tribes and were called *civitates*, literally cities, a term which in the ancient world included the city's territory. No such local government units are known north of Hadrian's Wall. A dedication to Jupiter, erected by the villagers settled at Fort Veluniate (Carriden at the east end of the Antonine Wall), however, reveals some form of local organization.

Documents from elsewhere in the empire reveal the nature of the involvement of the army in the administration of justice in a frontier zone. In Egypt this included dealing with a wide range of crimes such as theft, burglary, assault, arson, trespass and seeking missing persons.

One document from Vindolanda appears to relate to the administration of justice, though in this case the person seems to have been unable

to obtain it locally and is therefore appealing to a higher official, perhaps the governor. The fact that the man refers to himself as from overseas suggests that he is not a soldier.

> He beat[?] me all the more ... goods ... or pour them down the drain[?]. As befits an honest man[?] I implore your majesty not to allow me, an innocent man, to have been beaten with rods and, my lord, inasmuch as[?] I was unable to complain to the prefect because he was detained by ill-health, I have complained in vain[?] to the *beneficiarius* and the rest[?] of the centurions of his[?] unit. Accordingly[?] I implore your mercifulness not to allow me, a man from overseas and an innocent one, about whose good faith you may inquire, to have been bloodied by rods as if I had committed some crime.

This recalls St Paul's experience at Philippi where he was beaten and imprisoned uncondemned in spite of being a Roman citizen, and his question to the centurion after he had been tied up in the barracks in Jerusalem: 'Is it lawful for you to scourge a man who is a Roman citizen, and uncondemned?' Paul subsequently appeared before the Sanhedrin and then the governor of the province, before appealing to the emperor.

We have, perhaps, too favourable a view of the Roman world and the nature of the Roman peace. Brigandage, it would appear, was endemic within the Roman empire. To take just one example: at the time that his generals were winning victories in Britain in 206, the Emperor Septimius Severus lamented the fact that he was unable to capture a brigand terrorizing the Italian countryside. A fourth-century tombstone found at Ambleside in the Lake District refers to the killing of soldiers in the fort. Life may not have been as peaceful in northern Britain as we might like to believe.

Taxation

The army may also have helped collect customs duties at the frontier and taxes in the frontier area. Normally, within the Roman empire, taxes were paid in cash, but where the people were too poor these might be commuted to payment in kind. Thus in the early first century the Frisii on the north side of the Rhine had their taxation assessed in ox hides. There were no problems until the officer in charge of the collecting, by name Olennius, produced a new unit of measurement, the hide of a wild ox. This was larger than the hide of a domesticated animal and in effect resulted in an increase in taxation. In order to meet this burden the people sold their possessions and then their wives and children into slavery before eventually rising in revolt. The Batavians, another Rhineland tribe, had their taxation assessed in the form of recruits for the Roman army. It is possible that both methods of taxation operated in north Britain.

The new provincials might also suffer from requisition. This was a normal method of obtaining supplies for the army. Tacitus describes the abuse of this in the *Agricola*. He recorded that Agricola eased the levy of corn and the payment of tax by equalizing the burden and he abolished the devices invented by profiteers, which were more bitterly resented than the tax itself. The provincials had been compelled to wait outside locked granary doors and to buy back their corn at farcical prices. They were forced to deliver it by devious routes and to distant locations even though there were permanent quarters for troops close by. The description of the abuse almost obscures the fact that we see here requisitioning in practice. The army in fact paid, at set prices, for the goods it requisitioned and these prices might be greater than the current market value.

There were, however, other duties to pay. Tacitus places in Calgacus' mouth a number of grievances: conscription, tribute, the requisition of corn, and labour for the building of roads. Yet the local tribesmen must have paid taxation in some form. They were evidently not mere subsistence farmers, for the society in which they lived contained many non-producers who required feeding, such as warlords, priests,

architects and craftsmen. The Roman army might have displaced some of these people as the consumers of this surplus food, either through purchase or taxation. There is no evidence from coins or other artefacts reflecting the purchase of supplies on native sites. The dearth of such coins may be taken to suggest that goods obtained by the army were not paid for; alternatively, such coins as did exist may have gone to pay taxes. Perhaps, though, wealth was not measured in such terms. The local tribesmen may have counted their wealth in cattle, for example, just as today a large house or car might be taken as an indication of affluence.

Supplies

The Roman army in Scotland in both the first and second centuries was about 15,000-strong. These soldiers required enormous supplies of food and pottery, arms and armour, clothing and sleeping gear, medical supplies... the list is long. It also encompassed a wide variety of raw materials. Leather, for example, was far more important than today. It was used to make tents, saddles, shoes, clothing, purses, bags, shields and shield covers, hence the relevance of hides for taxation.

Wherever possible the army tried to obtain its supplies locally. Forts may have been located in river valleys, not because the surroundings were more congenial than bare moorland, but because the farms of the valleys would have offered food. It has been suggested that the underground passages (souterrains) attached to settlements (**colour plate 16**) provided storage for grain sold to the Roman army. Evidence that some food supplies were obtained locally comes from bones found on military sites. These are generally from adult and well-grown animals of the Celtic short-horn variety, the sort of animals which would have been found on the local farms. The bones were often split or smashed for marrow. In contrast, at Newstead many young animals were eaten while the bones were intact. Possibly here cattle

72 *Soldiers load tents on to a ship for transport along the Danube.*

were in greater supply. There were also indications of improved species.

Some food eaten at Bearsden, as we have seen, was imported from the Continent. None of the grain appears to have been grown locally, but was imported to the fort on the glume with final processing taking place on site.

It would appear that in the early third century the intention of Septimius Severus was not to rely upon local supplies but to keep his new forts in Scotland supplied from the south by sea (**72**). Both Cramond and Carpow were situated on the coast: to these two should be added a third, South Shields at the mouth of the River Tyne (see **87**). Here, on the site of an earlier fort, was built a supply base. Its fifteen granaries were of stone, implying that this site was to supply the forts of the permanent occupation of Scotland, not a brief campaign.

Documents from Britain and beyond demonstrate a network of military supply routes. Soldiers from Stobi in modern Bulgaria were apparently in Gaul in 105 collecting food. Surviving documents from the eastern provinces reveal that the armies of Cappadocia (in modern Turkey) and Judaea ordered clothing and blankets from Egypt and the army of Syria requisitioned camels in Egypt. Sabinus from Trier appears on one list at Vindolanda. Some items

might be delivered to the fort by suppliers. Receipts from the Fayum area of Egypt record the delivery of chaff for fuel to the fort at Dionysius in 301, while an order of similar date specifies the delivery of two horseloads of hay.

One of the longest documents found at Vindolanda concerns supply. Although none of the men mentioned in the document is specifically referred to as a soldier, the letter was found in the fort and a messmate (*contubernalis*) is mentioned. It reads:

Octavius to his brother Candidus, greetings. The 100 pounds of sinew from Marinus – I will settle up. From the time when you wrote about this matter, he has not even mentioned it to me. I have several times written to you that I have bought about 5000 *modii* of ears of grain, on account of which I need cash. Unless you send me some cash, at least 500 *denarii*, the result will be that I shall lose what I have laid out as a deposit, about 300 *denarii*, and I shall be embarrassed. So, I ask you, send me some cash as soon as possible. The hides which you write are at Cataractonium – write that they may be given to me and the wagon about which you write. And write to me what is with that wagon (**73**). I would have already been to collect them except that I did not care to injure the animals while the roads are bad. See with Tertius about the 8½ *denarii* which he received from Fatalis. He has not credited them to my account. Know that I have completed the 170 hides and I have the 119 *modii* of threshed *bracis* [a cereal used to make Celtic beer]. Make sure that you send me cash so that I may have ears of grain on the threshing floor. Moreover, I have already finished threshing all that I had. A messmate of our friend Frontius has been here. He was wanting me to allocate [?] him hides and that being so, was ready to give cash. I told him I would give him the hides by 1 March. He decided that he would come on 13 January. He did not turn up nor did he take any trouble to obtain them since he had hides. If he had given the cash, I would have given him them. I hear that Frontinius Iulius has for sale at a high price the leatherware[?] which he bought here for *5 denarii* apiece. Greet Spectatus and ... and Firmus. I have received letters from Gleuco. Farewell.

This single letter offers a remarkable insight into life on the northern frontier, supply and accounting: it has a very modern ring to it.

Soldiers might obtain items for themselves. The civil settlement was a ready source of goods. A fourth-century document from the eastern empire records payments by soldiers to the tailor, the fuller, the smith, for tunics and for a shield cover. Another source was the soldier's own family. Many letters from or to soldiers serving in eastern regiments demonstrate that clothing, arms and food were often sent to soldiers. Bread, wheat, barley, cake, cabbages, ceramons, fish, radish-oil, coconuts, a gourd and a citron are among the items requested or sent.

Letters from Vindolanda include several interesting references apparently to soldiers obtaining their own supplies. One records that, 'I have sent you....pairs of socks from Sattua, two pairs of sandals and two pairs of under-

pants, two pairs of sandals...' , another that 'a friend sent me fifty oysters from Cordonovi'.

What the soldiers could not obtain legally, they might obtain by extortion. In 238 the villagers of Scaptopara in Thrace complained that soldiers forced them to provide hospitality and supplies free of charge, while the complaints at Arague in Asia Minor a few years later included extortion, pillage and the theft of plough animals. A list of expenses drawn up by an agent for his master included the cost of wine for bribes to soldiers on several occasions. We have no evidence of such activities on the northern British frontier, but there is no reason to believe that they did not take place. However, the empire was founded on law and many officials strove to ensure that the laws were applied. Most emperors were assiduous in caring for their citizens and set a good example: the Emperor Domitian even bought the land on which to build forts in Germany.

Civil settlements

Soldiers always attract camp followers and the Roman army was no different. Each fort usually appears to have had its own civil settlement. It is possible that most of the people who lived in such villages in Scotland had followed the regiment when it moved north from its previous base. However, we know very little about such settlements. Earlier excavations revealed hearths outside the fort at Bar Hill and timber buildings at Cadder, both on the Antonine Wall. More recently, buildings of both timber and stone have been found outside the fort at Inveresk: fields, possibly of Roman date, lay beyond. Fields have also been recorded around the forts at Croy Hill and Carriden, but no buildings. Most intriguingly, investigations at Inveresk in 1995 led to the discovery of a building which, on plan, should be a Roman granary. It lies to the north of the ridge on which the fort sits, possibly on the former coastline: it may have been part of a harbour-warehouse complex (**74**). At Inveresk also, uniquely within Roman

73 *A cart wheel found at Newstead.*

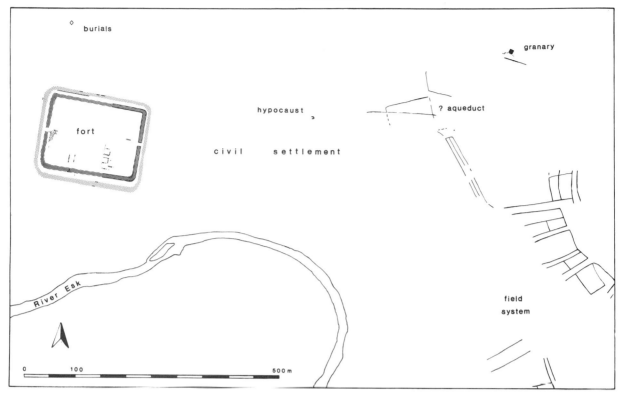

74 *The fort and civil settlement at Inveresk.*

Britain, have been found two inscriptions dedicated by an imperial procurator. Problems of supply may have brought this official, Q. Lusius Sabinianus, to Inveresk.

The army provided a lucrative market, for soldiers were relatively well paid. We have no inscriptions referring to merchants in Scotland, but such men certainly existed and are recorded elsewhere. A remarkable collection of dedications found at the mouth of the Rhine records thanks to the goddess Nehalannia for safe arrival after the sea voyage. These altars are dedicated by traders including a *negotiator Britannicianus* and a *negotiator cretarius Britannicianus* (a trader in fine pottery or pottery figurines).

The presence of the army also drew manufacturers to Scotland. Recent work has demonstrated that more pottery was made in Scotland than had previously been appreciated (**75**). A kiln has actually been found inside the fort at Bar Hill, but elsewhere the evidence comes from analysis of the type of pottery manufactured. In some cases we know the name of the potter. So many mixing bowls stamped with the name Sarrius have been found at Bearsden that it seems almost certain that this potter established a workshop outside that fort. Sarrius is known to have had workshops at two sites in England: he seems to have been an energetic businessman.

The civil settlement would also have contained temples (**76**). An inscription from Castlecary recorded the construction of a shrine to Mercury but its location is not known (see **8**). Beyond the civil settlement would have lain the cemetery. None has been excavated in Scotland, though tombstones and burials are known (**77, 78**). One burial cist at Camelon contained the remains of two bodies accompanied by weapons, while nearby a number of hollows may have been cremation pits.

Relations with local people

Although generally not in great numbers, Roman artefacts are found on native sites in

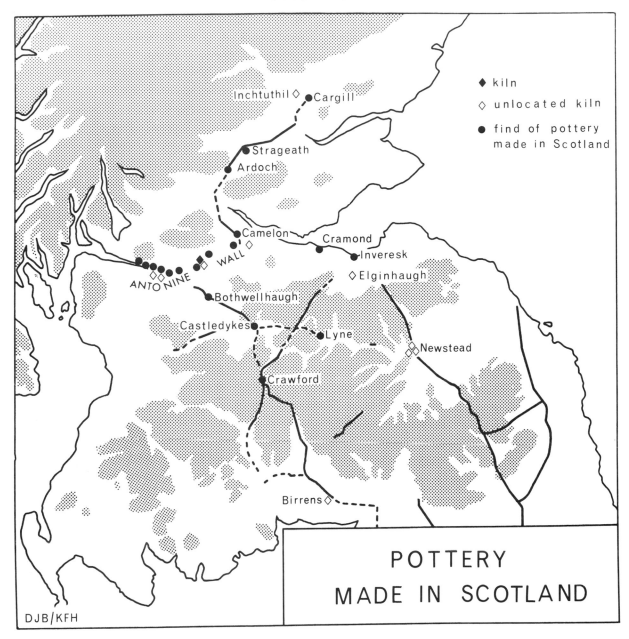

75 *A map indicating the find-spots of pottery made in Scotland.*

sufficient quantity for some conclusions to be made. Interestingly, there is a difference between the range of sites on which first-century and second-century artefacts appear. In the first century objects are mainly found on high-status sites, while in the second century they are found on a wider range of settlements.

This may suggest that only the upper echelons of society could obtain Roman goods in the first century, but the longer second-century occupation allowed these goods to trickle further down the social scale.

Sites which have furnished high-quality objects include Traprain Law and most of the excavated Lowland brochs (**colour plate 15**). Two brochs in particular, Buchlyvie and Leckie, have produced rich assemblages. Lesley

76 *The carving at the top of this altar from Birrens may be of the entrance to a temple.*

Macinnes has argued that Lowland brochs are not intrusive military structures, as has been proposed in the past, but are simply high-status dwellings built in the most modern style in order to emphasize the position of their owners. It is thus not surprising that they produce high-status, i.e. Roman, goods.

The impact of the Romans on the native people

It might be considered that the advent of the Romans would have had a major impact on the local people (**79**). Tacitus in the *Agricola* offered several examples of the impact of the Romans on Britain. These included changes in taxation and in land ownership, conscription into the army, the introduction of new architectural styles, education, language, dress, bathing, eating and religion. Several items in this list are not readily identifiable through

78 *An urn containing a cremation, buried at Newstead.*

77 *A funeral banquet recorded on a sepulchral relief found at Shirva on the Antonine Wall.*

79 *An artist's impression of a contemporary farmstead in south-west Scotland. Drawn by D. Pollock.*

excavation: taxation and ownership changes, education, language and conscription. There are others where archaeology could help: changes in farming practice, together with its effect on the landscape, changes in population distribution and in settlement patterns and population size, a growth in industry and mining, and changes in the structure of society. Indeed, the effect upon the structure of society must have been the most traumatic result of the arrival of the Romans. The local people were either soundly defeated by the Roman army and incorporated into a foreign State, or were faced by a formidable foe beyond their borders. Defeated leaders would have had to conform or be ousted. Ordinary people now had new masters to whom they must give obedience – and pay taxes. Leaders and led were now all second-class citizens.

It is not easy to find archaeological evidence in Scotland for the impact of the Romans on the local people. It has been proposed that the Roman peace led to the abandonment of hill-forts and also of defences around settlements (**colour plate 15**), an increase in the size of farms and settlements suggesting an increase in population, and changes in the use of building materials. In fact, none of these changes necessarily had anything to do with the Romans. Recent excavations have demonstrated that hill-forts had been abandoned long before. When the army came to lay out their targets

over the gates of the hill-fort at Burnswark (see **64**), its defences were in some disarray according to its excavator, George Jobey. Eildon Hill North does not appear to have been occupied at the time of the Roman advance, while excavation has also demonstrated that the defences of the settlement at Broxmouth in East Lothian had been abandoned before the Roman period. The increase in the size of farms and other settlements may have been related to the abandonment of hill-forts, as their inhabitants would presumably have had to find somewhere else to live.

Excavation, too, has suggested that the use of stone in the construction of houses may have started before the Romans arrived due to a scarcity of good timber for building. This is supported by evidence from the Roman period, for, as we have seen, the army frequently was unable to build with the best wood such as oak. The stone houses were round like their timber predecessors. There appears to have been no attempt to emulate Roman styles by constructing rectangular buildings.

It might be expected that the food requirements of the Roman army would have had a noticeable impact on the countryside, possibly with changes in farming practice. However, again, it would appear that the agricultural improvements of this time occurred before the arrival of the Romans.

In one way the presence of the Roman army does appear to have had an effect on the local people. It is interesting that the settlement hierarchy within the frontier zone is different, simpler, from that in the surrounding areas. Villas, with one possible exception, are not found in the military zone, though they occur just beyond it in Yorkshire. Beyond the military zone to the north are located brochs and souterrains (**colour plates 15 and 16**), the local equivalent of the high-status villas. Possibly in the frontier zone the army acted as an economic depressant, creaming off money from the local inhabitants, and replacing the local aristocracy as the elite of society, as indeed in one sense they were.

CHAPTER FIVE

Withdrawal

The Romans never maintained a permanent presence in Scotland, apart from on its most southerly fringes. Three times they established themselves in central Scotland and several times thereafter they invaded, but no episode lasted more than a generation or so. Why did they fail to maintain themselves in north Britain? First, let us look at the various withdrawals and the evidence for them.

In September 83 the army of Julius Agricola defeated a stronger Caledonian force at the battle of Mons Graupius and Agricola appears to have believed that he had defeated the main enemy in the north. About fifteen years later, his son-in-law, Tacitus, remarked that 'Britain was conquered and immediately abandoned'. While this may have been directed at the frontier policy of the Emperor Domitian and include some hyperbole, nevertheless its core is correct: the Caledonians had been defeated but the victory had not been sustained.

Excavations at the legionary base at Inchuthil have demonstrated that the fortress was abandoned even before it was completed (see **39**). No house for the legionary legate had been constructed and open spaces existed elsewhere within the perimeter of the ramparts. At Inchtuthil and other forts in the north, coins of 86 have been found, but not of 87, a year when they were produced in equal abundance. This indicates that these northern forts were abandoned within the period after the arrival of the coins of 86 but before those of 87 could reach

this north-west frontier. Mid-88 thus appears to be the latest date at which the regiments were withdrawn. The withdrawal did not just affect Inchtuthil and its surrounding installations, but all forts north and west of a line running from Newstead in Tweeddale to Glenlochar near Castle Douglas in the Ken valley.

Striking evidence for the withdrawal was discovered at Inchtuthil. Buried in pits in the legionary workshop were found ¾ ton (0.762 tonnes) of nails, all unused (**80**). They were

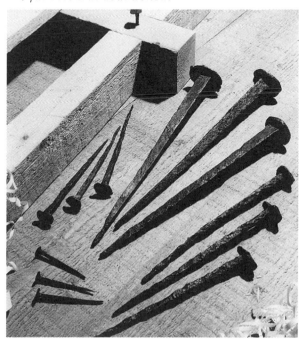

80 *Some of the nails buried at Inchtuthil when the fortress was abandoned.*

presumably abandoned because it was not worth the effort of carrying them south, and buried so as to deny their use to the local tribesmen. The action of burial points to an ordered withdrawal. Generally, fort buildings were demolished and burnt by the Roman army. Such burning in the past has frequently been interpreted as evidence for destruction by the enemy. Sometimes it is not possible to tell the agent of destruction, but occasionally bent nails point to the demolition of buildings before the conflagration and support the evidence for orderly withdrawal. Fort ramparts might be slighted, but not completely demolished as the surviving remains demonstrate (see **83**).

What led to the abandonment of Agricola's conquests? In 85 and in 86 the Romans suffered crushing defeats on the Danube. The strong Dacian kingdom, centred on modern Transylvania, was powerful enough to challenge the might of Rome and successful enough, in the meantime, to sustain that challenge. No less than three Roman armies were defeated by Decebalus and his Dacians before a peace was patched up. In order to strengthen the frontier forces on the Danube, *legio II Adiutrix* was withdrawn from Britain. It may have moved as early as the winter of 85/6: it was certainly on the Danube by 93. Some auxiliary units probably accompanied the legion.

This was a significant loss for the army of Britain. The legion alone represented about an eighth of its strength. If a similar number of auxiliary regiments left too, then the provincial army was reduced by up to a quarter. Considering that Wales, northern England and southern Scotland had been conquered within the space of fourteen years, it is not surprising that the army preferred to ensure that it effectively consolidated its hold on the core conquests even if this resulted in the abandonment of the periphery.

In effect, those territories abandoned in 87/8 were those conquered by Agricola himself, hence Tacitus' comment. We have seen that Cerialis appears to have built a fort at Carlisle

and probably made contact with tribes further north. Thus, in withdrawing to a line just north of the Cheviots, the army was perhaps retreating to the position reached by Cerialis more than twelve years before.

The new line was strange (**81**: cf **38**). Within north Britain the most obvious line to hold within the island is the Forth–Clyde isthmus. After that comes the Tyne–Solway isthmus, twice as long: Hadrian's Wall was 80 Roman miles long, the Antonine Wall 40 Roman miles. Between the two, the modern Anglo-Scottish border utilizes the Cheviot Hills.

The Roman line of the late first century lay not on the Cheviots, but a little to the north. The forts known to have been occupied at this time lay on an axis from Newstead in Tweeddale through Oakwood in Ettrickdale, Milton in Annandale, Dalswinton in Nithsdale to Glenlochar in the Ken valley. All these forts have produced two types of evidence to support occupation at this time. This evidence takes the form of the structural remains of a second phase of occupation in the Flavian period and artefacts of late first-century date. Other forts to the north have furnished one type of evidence but not the other. There is late first-century pottery at Castlecary on the Forth–Clyde isthmus, a site lying on the watershed between the Forth and Clyde river systems. There is structural evidence for a second Flavian period at two sites, Loudon Hill to the west and Elginhaugh to the east. At Elginhaugh the fort was abandoned after a single period of occupation, but its site was then used for another purpose. Some of the fort gates were modified while ditches were dug across the annexe apparently focused on its entrance. The excavator, Bill Hanson, has suggested that it may have served as a collecting point for animals supplied to the army.

It is difficult to interpret the evidence for occupation at these sites. Possibly they were outposts beyond the main line; perhaps there are other forts of this date waiting to be discovered. Certainly it reminds us that the

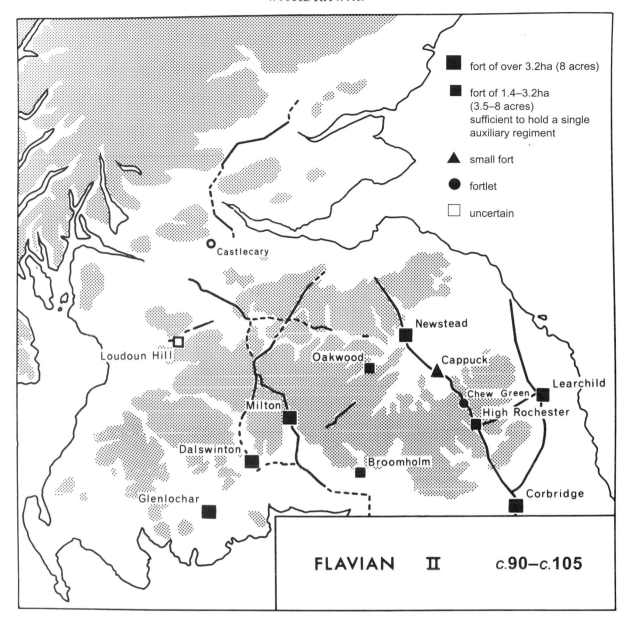

81 *Forts occupied in north Britain in the late first century after the withdrawal from the north.*

Romans did not see boundaries in the way that we see them today, definitively marking the frontiers between equal sovereign States.

While a line can be drawn on a map from Newstead to Glenlochar, and roads linked the forts, this again was not necessarily how the Romans saw the situation. The main forts of Newstead, Milton, Dalswinton and Glenlochar were all situated in major river valleys. The Romans may have seen the forts simply as convenient bases to control the people living in

these valleys. The availability of forces did not allow them to retain a fort in Clydesdale, where Castledykes was abandoned, nor as far north as the Forth basin.

There is another point worthy of consideration. The Romans regarded client States as part of their empire: Augustus' record of his own achievements makes this clear. The

Brigantes had been established as a client State soon after the invasion of 43, and were only formally incorporated into the province when Cartimandua, Queen of the Brigantes and Rome's ally, had been thrown out of her territory by rebels. Thus, to retreat further south than the Tyne–Solway in 87/8 would have been to abandon land regarded as Roman for forty years. Seen in that light, the forts beyond Brigantia were merely outposts, shielding the province from unexpected attack.

The Tyne–Solway line

In the event, the occupation of Newstead and its fellows was not to be permanent. No earlier than 103 (from coin evidence), a new phase of occupation commenced at Corbridge and the abandonment of the more northerly sites has been linked to this. The existing forts on the Tyne–Solway isthmus were modified and new ones added. This was the line to be taken by Hadrian's Wall twenty years later.

We have no evidence to indicate the reason for this further withdrawal. It appears to have occurred in the early years of the Emperor Trajan (98–117). He was responsible for the extension of the empire on the lower Danube through his conquest of the Dacians and the incorporation of their kingdom into the empire. Trajan's first Dacian war commenced in 103 and it is possible that the retreat to the Tyne–Solway line was the result of yet more troop withdrawals from the island in order to strengthen the army on the Danube in preparation for war.

On both occasions, in 87/8 and about 103, the withdrawal from forts in southern and eastern Scotland appears to have been the result of problems elsewhere in the empire. This is not to say that there were no conditions in Britain which forced withdrawal. The speed of conquest in the 70s and 80s was not conducive to stability. The troops to occupy the more northerly forts were themselves withdrawn from areas relatively recently conquered while the Boudican revolt, less than twenty

years before, cannot have been far from the thoughts of decision makers. Wales and the north, too, was not easy territory to hold. It was mountainous and fragmented, creating difficulties for an occupying force. The cautious approach, 'last in, first out', had much to commend it in the circumstances.

Furthermore, we should not forget the references to warfare in Britain during the reigns of Trajan and Hadrian, in particular the award of military decorations under Trajan and the statement at the time of Hadrian's accession that the Britons could not be held under Roman control (see Chapter 6). Perhaps the Romans did not have it all their own way!

The Antonine withdrawal

The exact date of the withdrawal from the Antonine Wall is not known. A lost inscription dating to 158 recording repair work on Hadrian's Wall suggests that the intention then was to bring that frontier back into commission. There is much to be said for linking the break in occupation between the two periods of second-century occupation of Scotland to that date. This is supported by an inscription recording the rebuilding of Birrens in the same year, while Brough-on-Noe in Derbyshire was rebuilt at about the same time, pointing to a wholesale reappraisal of the British frontier.

Whatever the intention was, however, it was not fully implemented. Excavations at Crawford and at Newstead have shown that there was no appreciable break between the two Antonine phases. We do not, cannot, know the reason for the apparent decision to withdraw from Scotland in the mid-150s. Local unrest among the tribes has been suggested, and linked to a coin issue of 154 supposedly showing Britannia subdued (**82**). This, however, is four years before 158. A destruction layer between the two Antonine periods at Birrens has been interpreted as evidence for hostile action. It is possible though that the destruction was caused by the Roman

82 *Coin of 154 showing* Britannia *on the reverse.*

army itself who frequently destroyed its buildings when changing the regiment. Perhaps a decision to withdraw from Scotland, taken by the governor Julius Verus (155–8), was reversed on instructions from Rome.

The next decision to withdraw was not reversed. A coin found in a granary at Old Kilpatrick remains the best *terminus post quem.* The coin was struck between 164 and 169 and has been described as 'fairly worn'. Pottery is held to support a date for withdrawal about 163: later second-century samian pottery is found in Scotland, but only on civilian not on military sites. It is most unlikely that concrete evidence will be found to help determine the date of abandonment: the best we can hope for is further refinement of the archaeological dating evidence.

In the circumstances, therefore, we again have to rely upon an appreciation of the historical situation to help determine a date and reason for abandonment. A recent reappraisal of the evidence by Charles Daniels draws attention to the energetic frontier policy of Marcus which led him to extend the empire on the eastern frontier, and consider new provinces beyond the Danube. Only a most serious situation would surely have led to retraction in Britain. Daniels suggests that such a situation occurred in the late 160s when there was a serious problem on the Danube exacerbated by an outbreak of plague. 168–9 thus offers a historical context for the abandonment of the Antonine Wall. Even so, there are later coins from the line of the Wall, and a probable later inscription from Castlecary (see 8), indicating subsequent activity in the area.

As the army withdrew it appears to have demolished its own installations. The distance-slabs on the Antonine Wall were buried then, if not in 158. Architectural fragments, altars and weapons were tipped down fort wells or buried in pits. Timber buildings were burnt, fort ramparts slighted (83).

Withdrawal from Scotland entailed the recommissioning of Hadrian's Wall. The forts were repaired, the milecastles and turrets restored, the Vallum cleaned out. As far as we can see, the Wall was restored to the state it had been in when abandoned in the early 140s, with one difference. At this time a road appears to have been added to the frontier. This road for part of its length lay close to the line of a possible predecessor along the north berm of the Vallum, but it was certainly a new structure. Its construction may have been the result of experiencing the advantages of the road built immediately beside the Antonine Wall.

83 *The band of burning in front of the east rampart of the fort at Bearsden. This contained fragments of willow and alder branches and may have been the rampart's breastwork thrown down and burnt when the fort was abandoned.*

84 *A face-jar, probably of the Emperor Caracalla (211–17).*

The Severan withdrawal

The abandonment of the conquests of the Emperor Septimius Severus by his son Caracalla (84), following his father's death in York on 4 February 211, is the only occasion when the details of a withdrawal are given. According to Cassius Dio, Caracalla 'made treaties with the enemy, evacuated their territory and abandoned the forts', departing for Rome. This was certainly sensible from Caracalla's point of view. He was only the second emperor of the dynasty and it behoved him to consolidate his position – not least in relation to his younger and popular brother – by returning to Rome, the centre of power. This did not in itself necessitate abandonment of the recent conquests. The new Emperor Commodus had done the same fifty years before, following the death of his father, Marcus Aurelius, when he abandoned his father's expensively won conquests in

Germany. Possibly in both cases this was a reaction to the fathers rather than to the particular situation. Nor can we be certain how quickly the previous policy was overturned. Two phases of building have been recorded at Carpow, suggesting at least more than a single season's occupation, while an inscription from the site appears to refer to a single emperor and therefore ought to date after the murder of Geta in 212 (85). Cramond has produced third-century pottery indicating continuing occupation. Paul Bidwell and Stephen Speak, in their reappraisal of the dating of the supply base at South Shields, have suggested that the Fifth Cohort of Gauls did not return from Cramond until 222–35.

Why did the Romans fail to conquer northern Scotland?

This question has vexed the minds of many. How was it that one of the world's greatest armies failed to complete the conquest of

85 *Part of an early third-century inscription found at Carpow.*

Britain? Were the people too ferocious to conquer? Were the mountains too vast to control? Did the Romans decide there was no economic gain in holding north Britain? Was the social, political and economic infrastructure of the northern tribes insufficiently advanced to aid their easy absorption into the empire? Were the supply lines to the north too tenuous? Did imperial politics militate against conquest? Did the Romans embark upon the conquest of Britain too late in their history? As usual, the truth is probably a mixture of all these factors.

Caledonian fighters

The Caledonians would appear to have been doughty fighters. Dio stated that they stood their ground with great determination and Herodian that they were fearsome and dangerous fighters, though of course it was in the Romans' interest to exaggerate the fighting qualities of their opponents.

It took Agricola two years to bring the Caledonians to defeat at Mons Graupius and at first they had the better of the war, surprising the Roman army by attacking one of its forts and then nearly destroying the ninth legion in a night attack on its camp. In fact, we would have a rather different view of Agricola if the Caledonians had been successful in this attack, or if he had been withdrawn at the end of that season rather than the next.

Severus at the end of his first campaign thought that he had conquered the Caledonians, only to have them rise against him. During both wars, the Caledonians appear to have adopted guerrilla tactics, their most sensible approach to the discipline of the Roman army, though in neither case ultimately successful.

A document from Vindolanda offers a rather different perspective of the fighting tactics of the Britons. It records that 'the Britons are unprotected by armour[?]. There are very many cavalry. The cavalry do not use swords nor do the wretched Britons mount in order to throw javelins.' Interestingly, Tacitus had stated that the main strength of the Britons was in their infantry. Unfortunately we know no more about this document: it may have been an intelligence report, or a comment by the training officer. It is certainly pejorative in its use of the word 'Brittunculi', wretched or little Britons.

During the first and second centuries senior and experienced generals were sent to govern Britain, supported by a strong army. It might be argued that this was because it faced a particularly warlike opponent. It may be, however, that the army was necessary simply because the Caledonians were unconquered, not unconquerable. Conquest of the northern part of the island would presumably, in time, have allowed the Romans to reduce the size of their army in Britain, as they had done in Spain. But Spain had taken 200 years to conquer, albeit under the very different conditions of the republic. Two hundred years from the invasion of 43 brings us to 243, in the middle of the civil wars and upset of the third century. By that time Rome was no longer capable of sustaining a war of conquest. Its capability in Britain was further restricted by a reduction in the size of the army in the island.

Caledonian mountains

The Highlands of Scotland are certainly an impressive massif. Today, vast and barren, often the only trees are those planted by the Forestry Commission. Their predecessors had been cleared 2000 years before the Romans arrived, in the Neolithic and early Bronze Ages, leaving only isolated pockets of the original pine and birch woods.

The Scottish Highlands have many mountains rising to 1000m (3000ft), but few over 1300m (4000ft). In both extent and height, this mountainous area is matched elsewhere in the empire. The mountains of Dalmatia, for example, are both more extensive and higher. All such mountainous areas, whether in Spain, Dalmatia, Asia Minor or the Alps, caused the Roman army considerable trouble, but in all cases the people of these areas were ultimately conquered. It is difficult to see why the Scottish Highlands would have been any different. The climate was not the same as other mountainous areas, but the climate of the Anatolian plateau, for example, had its own problems.

Furthermore, the people of the Scottish Highlands were conquered by a later imperial power, Hanoverian Britain. While such parallels are never exact, there are some similarities in the relations between the Romans and the Hanoverians on the one hand and the Caledonians and Highland clansmen on the other. Both were clashes between the techni-

cally superior, better disciplined and better armed permanent armies of external imperial forces and irregularly armed local tribesmen only trained through the framework of tribal warfare, which may have operated according to its own conventions.

Interestingly, the pattern of control established by the Hanoverian army was little different from that which we might have expected the Romans to impose in similar circumstances (86). Major

86 *Map of eighteenth-century Hanoverian forts and roads in Scotland.*

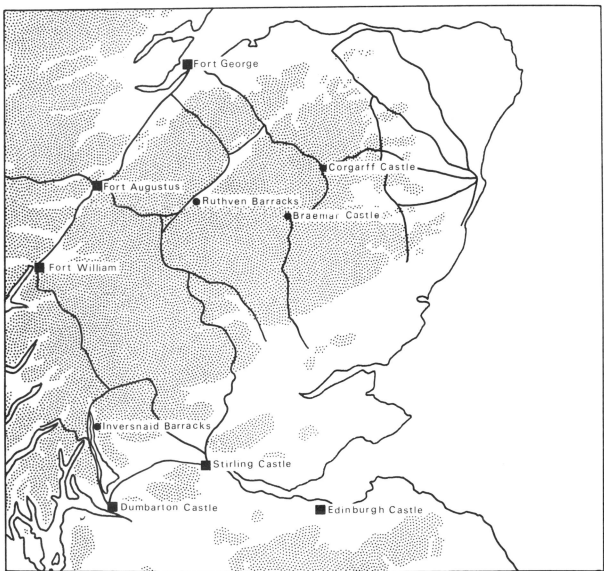

forts were established in the main river valleys, in this case the Great Glen where Forts George, Augustus and William were built. The garrison of Fort George was two regiments, the same as Newstead in Tweeddale. Between these forts and the main bases surrounding the Highlands – Dumbarton, Stirling, Blackness and Edinburgh – were barracks, or fortlets, such as Corgarff, Braemar and Ruthven. All were linked by roads. In a conscious acknowledgement of earlier activities, the builder of many of these roads, General Wade, placed an inscription in Latin on his bridge at Aberfeldy recording that he had built 150 miles (240km) of roads beyond the limits of the Roman empire. It may not be too far-fetched to conclude that what was possible for the Hanoverians would have been possible for the Romans.

Economic advantages

It is difficult to believe that the conquest of Scotland would have brought any economic gain to Rome. It was not rich in minerals or agricultural produce: on the other hand it is not clear if the presence of these would have affected Rome's attitude to the north. We have already seen that Rome considered that she had a right to rule the world. In that way, her attitude of mind was rather similar to that of the western European countries in the nineteenth century. Suetonius, in describing why Claudius invaded Britain, stated simply that the emperor required a triumph: no mention of acquiring minerals, agricultural produce, nor even British hunting dogs.

Economic reasons were adduced by some writers to explain why Rome did not conquer a particular area. Strabo, for example, remarked that more seemed to accrue from customs duties on commerce with Britain than direct taxation could supply, if the cost of maintaining an army to garrison the island and collecting the tribute was deducted. Yet, a generation later, Claudius was to invade Britain – because he required a triumph. Possibly

Strabo's explanation of why Augustus failed to follow up the exploits of his uncle, Julius Caesar, in Britain is not really a reason but an excuse. A hundred years after Claudius, Aelius Aristides claimed that Rome held all that was worth having and Appian, a former *advocatus fisci* (financial secretary to the emperor), remarked that the Romans ruled the most important part of the island and had no need of the rest: 'in fact, the part they have brings in little money'. But, again, is this a reason or an excuse? It is worth noting that both Aelius Aristides and Appian were Greeks and accordingly did not have the same forthright view of imperialism as the Romans. Yet economic considerations do not appear to have been a major concern for the Romans, though it must be acknowledged that the acquisition of booty could be of interest to them. That, however, may not have been such a consideration in north Britain.

Social and economic infrastructure

It has been argued that the social and economic infrastructure of the northern tribes was insufficiently developed for Rome to impose her own type of local self-government on them successfully. The tribes of northern England and Scotland certainly had no coinage of their own, unlike their compatriots in southern Britain, and in manufacturing terms, such as pottery and metalwork, they were not so advanced. Yet they were not without social and political sophistication. They were organized into tribes, probably headed by kings: a king of the Orkneys is mentioned. They had the political framework to organize the land. Theirs was not a subsistence economy, but an agricultural regime capable of producing surpluses to feed the ruling class, the priests and craftsmen. Some of their constructions survive to this day, including the dry-stone-built broch of Mousa, still standing 13m (40ft) high after weathering 2000 years of Shetland storms and two sieges in Norse times. Moreover, architectural skills

87 *Aerial view showing several of the granaries in the base at South Shields at the mouth of the River Tyne probably built by the Emperor Septimius Severus in order to help supply his newly planned forts in Scotland.*

were not new to these people: the chambered tomb at Maeshowe was over 2500 years old by the time of the Agricolan advance.

One of the greatest political tests the Caledonians had to face occurred in 83 when they were confronted by the threat posed by the Roman advance. Then, they were able to combine their forces and choose leaders for their army. That they failed is immaterial: the correct political as well as military decision had been taken.

Supply

It is possible that the occupation of Scotland would have overstretched the supply lines of the Roman army. There is some evidence for this in that the Emperor Septimius Severus appears to have established a supply base at South Shields at the mouth of the Tyne, probably in order to help maintain his projected northern conquests rather than just aid the short-lived campaigns (87). This might suggest that it was held that insufficient supplies could have been obtained locally for the regiments newly established in Scotland. Yet the land of north-east Scotland appears to have been able to support a sizeable population, one certainly capable of standing up to Agricola at Mons Graupius.

Imperial politics

The events on the northern frontier did not take place in a vacuum. As we have seen, it was the emperor who decided where the boundary of the empire should be and who would have ordered advance or withdrawal. In 82 it was presumably Domitian who instructed Agricola to resume his march north, and the same emperor who effectively terminated the advance by withdrawing a legion from Britain for service on the Danube. The next stage in the retreat may have been related to further troop withdrawals. Hadrian's reign saw maintenance of the status quo in Britain.

The advance under Antoninus Pius between 139 and 142 is particularly illuminating. Firstly, it appears to have been engineered simply in order for the new emperor to gain military prestige. Secondly, it was most certainly not an attempt to complete the conquest of the whole island. In fact the new territory was even more limited in extent than Agricola's northern conquests (**88**; cf **38**), and this underlines the specific purpose of the action. Similarly, the withdrawal twenty-five years later may have related to imperial politics.

88 *Military deployment in Scotland in the mid-second century.*

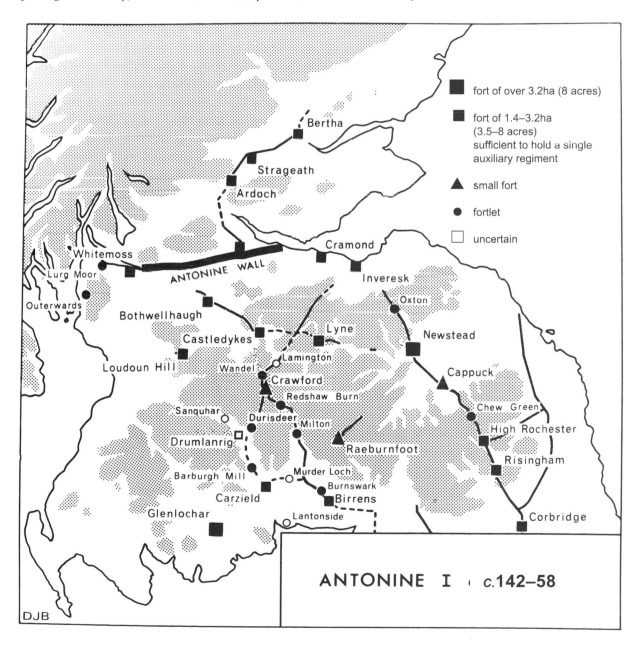

Finally, the Severan advance was undertaken at the behest of the emperor, because he liked fighting, the army needed stiffening and his sons taking away from the flesh-pots of Rome, and, almost as an afterthought, there was trouble on the northern frontier. It ended with the death of the emperor and the not unreasonable desire of his successor to consolidate his power in Rome.

Certain factors governed actions on the northern frontier. Firstly, the emperor had to be interested. Vespasian, Domitian, Antoninus Pius and Severus were both interested and concerned to extend the frontier northwards. Titus does not appear to have been interested, nor Trajan and Hadrian, and certainly not Caracalla. Secondly, there had to be no activities elsewhere to distract attention or resources. Serious problems closer to the heart of the empire were given preference and, as a result, troops were often withdrawn from Britain, even at critical moments. Even while Agricola was fighting at Mons Graupius some of his army had been detached for service in the German war. The location of Britain on the edge of the Roman world worked to her disadvantage. For the people of the island it brought them Roman attention, since crossing Oceanus and conquering the land on the edge of the world brought particular prestige to leaders such as Claudius and Julius Caesar, who received more days' triumph for his foray into Britain than for the conquest of Gaul. Once Britain was within the Roman domain, the location of the island ensured that it was rarely top of an emperor's agenda. Ironically, at the one time when most of the factors were favourable – peace on other frontiers and an interested emperor – Antoninus Pius' specific aim seems to have been very limited and too closely related to his own problems.

Conclusion

It might be expected that several factors played a part in the Romans' failure to maintain their hold on southern Scotland and to conquer the north. The opposition of the Caledonian tribes ensured that the advance would be strongly opposed. The nature of the Scottish Highlands must have been a discouragement: perhaps this lay behind the decision to halt on the Forth–Clyde line in 80. The apparent lack of any economic benefit is probably of some relevance, as is the relative backwardness of the tribes which would have rendered their incorporation into the political structures of the empire more difficult. Perhaps the problems of extended supply lines were significant. Nor was the situation helped by Britain's location on the very edge of the known world. When trouble occurred elsewhere, it took precedence. Perhaps if the tribes had not been so warlike, the mountains so high, the lack of economic benefit so obvious, the geographical and social difficulties so great, Rome might have triumphed. But in addition to the local factors, the political circumstances within the empire rarely combined to allow the Roman army to advance northwards. As a result, Scotland remained frontier country, most of it beyond the empire, but with whom the empire still had a relationship.

CHAPTER SIX

External relations

Scotland, for most of the Roman period, lay beyond the empire, not a unified country but a land occupied by independent States. We only know the names of these States from Roman sources. Ptolemy, presumably obtaining his information from the Agricolan campaigns, listed twelve tribes north of the Tyne–Solway isthmus (see **28**) and to these we can perhaps add the kingdom of the Orcades: the fourth-century writer Eutropius stated that its king submitted to Claudius in 43. The Maeatae appeared about 200 (**89**) and the Picts a century later. So far we have been examining Roman aggressive actions, but the Caledonians were not inactive themselves.

Caledonian invasions

The Caledonians opposed the Roman invasion from the very beginning, and the States of southern Scotland may not have been such an easy conquest as we often suppose. Thereafter, there are many references and hints, most rather enigmatic, to trouble on the northern frontier.

Military decorations were awarded to a unit and an officer either in the late first or early second century for meritorious conduct in Britain. *Cohors I Cugernorum*, stationed in Britain, was awarded the title *Ulpia Traiana* and a grant of Roman citizenship to all its soldiers during the reign of Trajan (98–117) apparently for a particular military exploit, while the commander of *cohors II Austurum*

was decorated in a British war some time between 105 and about 125. When Hadrian succeeded as emperor in 117, we are told that the Britons could not be kept under Roman control, while Cornelius Fronto, writing in 162, in a throw-away remark, commented that many soldiers were killed by the Britons during Hadrian's reign. All these references are frustratingly vague, but all indicate warfare in Britain, perhaps on the northern frontier.

Pausanias' comment in his *Description of Greece* that 'Antoninus Pius appropriated most of the territory of the Brigantes because they had begun a war, invading Genunia, which is subject to the Romans' is no clearer. The Brigantes lived within the empire and therefore could hardly invade it, unless Pausanias was referring to those Brigantes who lived beyond the west end of Hadrian's Wall; perhaps, however, he simply got his terminology wrong.

This hint that the southern Scottish tribes were not necessarily as peaceful as usually presumed does receive some support from a late second-century inscription found at Kirksteads at the west end of Hadrian's Wall. The stone was erected by the commander of *legio VI Victrix* to give thanks for 'the successful outcome of action conducted beyond the Wall'. A regimental commander dedicated an altar at Corbridge after slaughtering a band of Corionototae, who are otherwise unattested. In the fourth century a tombstone at Ambleside

89 *The independent States and Roman* civitates *of north Britain about 200.*

records the death of one soldier, perhaps two, 'killed in the fort by the enemy'.

The latter part of the second and the early years of the third century saw a series of disturbances in Britain. At the beginning of the reign of Marcus and Lucius in 161 'war was threatening in Britain... and Calpurnius Agricola was sent to deal with the Britons'. In 169/70 'the Britons were on the verge of war'. The next reign commenced with a major invasion when 'the tribes in the island crossed the wall that separated them from the Roman legions, did a great deal of damage, and cut down a general and his troops'. In 197 the governor of Britain was not sufficiently strong, presumably because of the civil war, to mount an offensive against the Maeatae and Caledonians and therefore 'bought peace for a considerable sum of money'. Ten years later, his successor was 'winning wars in Britain'. It is not clear how we should regard the reasons given for the Severan invasions of 209–11. It may be that the governor of the province could have dealt with the situation by himself, but in the event the emperor decided to intervene for his own reasons.

The third century is generally regarded as peaceful, but that may simply reflect the paucity of the sources for the period. The beginning of the fourth century saw the rise of a new threat in the north, the Picts.

The rise of the Picts

A hundred years separated the Severan invasions of Scotland from those of Constantius Chlorus in 305. During that period the Roman empire suffered from civil wars and invasions. No one at the time could have foreseen that the advent of a new emperor, Diocletian, in 285 would bring about such momentous changes. He ended the civil wars, reformed the army, civil service and economy, divided the empire into two, and created a system of succession so far lacking. He also had the distinction of being the only emperor to abdicate. That action revealed that his system of succession ignored human weaknesses, in particular the desire of fathers for sons to succeed them. The arrangements for succession soon fell apart and the eventual victor was Constantine the Great.

Table 3
Family tree of Constantine the Great

Constantius Chlorus
Caesar of the western empire 286–305
Emperor 305–6
Campaigned against Picts 305
Died at York 306

▼

Constantine I (the Great)
Declared emperor at York 306
Campaigned against Picts 312?
Died 337

▼

Constans I
Emperor 337–61
Came to Britain winter 342/3

The House of Constantine (**table 3**) was to have a close relationship with Britain. Constantius Chlorus, founder of the dynasty, campaigned against the Picts in 305, though we do not know why. He died at York the following summer. His son, declared emperor by the British army, spent the next twenty years fighting his rivals before becoming sole emperor in 324, and a Christian on his deathbed in 337 (**colour plate 2**). He came to Britain in 312 and probably also campaigned against the Picts. It seems that Constantine was responsible for withdrawing the regiments from the outpost forts of Hadrian's Wall, Bewcastle, Netherby, Risingham and High Rochester, presumably in order to help him fight his rivals. The reason for his invasion of Pictland is not known.

Ammianus Marcellinus, in describing events on the northern frontier, remarked that Constans came to Britain in the winter of 342/3. The reason is not given, but the context suggests trouble on the frontier. Ammianus Marcellinus certainly made clear that the Picts were causing problems for the Romans. In 360 'the Scots and the Picts carried out raids, having disrupted the agreed peace, and laid waste places near the frontiers'. Reinforcements led by Lupicinus, a senior general, were sent to Britain. In 364 Ammianus recorded that the Picts, Saxons, Scots and Attacotti, an otherwise unknown people, 'harassed Britain in a never-ending series of disasters'. In 367 these peoples once more invaded the province, killing the Count of the Saxon Shore, and circumventing the military commander in the north. Again, an army had to be sent from the Continent, led by another senior general, Theodosius. He defeated the invaders, restored forts, 'protected the frontiers with sentries and forts', and disbanded the frontier scouts who had betrayed the Romans to their enemies.

Theodosius may have defeated the Picts and Scots on this occasion, but he had not quelled them permanently. Magnus Maximus in 382 'conducted a vigorous campaign, in which he defeated the Picts and Scots, who had carried out an invasion'. At the end of the next decade, Stilicho, the virtual ruler of the empire, is credited with defending Britain against the Scots, Picts and Saxons.

The whole tenor of the accounts of the relationship between the Romans and their northern neighbours in the fourth century indicates that the pendulum had swung against Rome. Now Rome was incapable of mounting a war of conquest. The invasions described above appear to have been reactive or punitive expeditions resulting in withdrawal as soon as the immediate task had been achieved.

Roman defence

Throughout most of the 300 and more years that the Romans maintained a frontier in north Britain, they also maintained a strong army there. During the reign of Hadrian (117–38) the size of the army in north Britain can be estimated as two legions and about fifty auxiliary regiments. The army was strengthened in 175 by the sending of 5500 Sarmatians to the island following the conclusion of a peace treaty on the Danube frontier.

There is evidence subsequently for a reduction in the size of the army, perhaps as a result of peaceful conditions on the northern frontier. The series of inscriptions from the forts of north Britain ends in the middle of the third century and when we next have good evidence for the location of units, in the late Roman army list known as the *Notitia Dignitatum* which dates to about 400, there were new units in many of the forts behind Hadrian's Wall. These regiments were creations of the army remodelled by Diocletian and Constantine. It is probable that they did not arrive in Britain until the early fourth century and are presumably a response to the increasing threat posed by the Picts. The Romans were paying a price for their ancestors' failure to conquer Scotland! The army, which had fallen to about 22 regiments in the north, was increased to about 37. There was a difference, though, for while the units of the second century were, theoretically, either 1000- or 500-strong, those of the fourth century were much smaller, containing perhaps little more than 100 men. In the last years of the century further reinforcements arrived in the shape of a field army which was established in Britain.

Rome also sent highly qualified governors to Britain throughout the first and second centuries. These men were often the top generals of their day. They included Statius Priscus, recalled from Britain after less than a year to take command in Cappadocia against the Parthians, and Julius Severus, also sent right across the empire, to lead the armies against the Jewish rebels in 132. The presence of these generals in Britain is a testimony to the conditions on the northern frontier, and also the size of the army which required a commander of appropriate rank. There is another factor. The fact that Britain is an island would have made the sending of reinforcements difficult. Hence a rather larger garrison may have been maintained here than was strictly required.

The frontier zone

The States of north Britain presumably had distinct boundaries, though these cannot be recognized today. Roman military measures for the defence of their northern frontier have certainly obscured these boundaries for none of the linear barriers, nor indeed other arrangements, seems to have respected tribal territory. The lack of coincidence between military and tribal boundaries is not surprising. Roman military installations were located with specific considerations in mind. One of these was the protection of the province, whose boundary presumably marched with those of the tribes on the frontier. Another was the use of convenient geographical features. Hadrian's Wall utilized the Whin Sill in the central sector, but to the east and west it also usually followed lines with wide views, especially to the north.

The Antonine Wall lay on the south lip of the central valley of Scotland for much of its length, again with wide views to the north.

The linear boundaries themselves were, however, only one part of the frontier installations, which included outpost forts as well as forts to the south stretching as far as the legionary bases at York and Chester. In the late first century, the most northern bases lay beyond the Cheviots. After these had been abandoned and Hadrian's Wall built, forts still lay beyond the barrier. Three stations at Bewcastle, Netherby and Birrens, apparently planned from the first to be part of the new frontier complex, possibly protected that part of the Brigantes sundered from the rest of the province by the construction of the Wall (**90**, see **43**).

On the return to Hadrian's Wall following the abandonment of the Antonine frontier, the same outpost forts were reoccupied and were joined by two more on the eastern side of the country, Risingham and High Rochester (see **91**). Birrens was later abandoned, probably about 180, leaving four outpost forts. Each appears to have been the base for a large regiment, the 1000-strong mixed infantry and cavalry unit. In the early third century some of these regiments were supplemented by irregular units, sometimes resulting in the basing of three units at one site. The forts were too small to hold such bodies of men and it seems that some must have been outposted. One outpost appears to have lain in the vicinity of Jedburgh where two Roman inscriptions have been found in the medieval abbey. So far as we can tell, this base lay deep into Votadinian territory.

On other frontiers Rome sought to maintain a cleared zone beyond the strict limit of empire. There is no evidence for this in Britain. There is, though, a hint that military units were raised in the frontier area. Ten *numeri* (irregular units) of *Brittones* are known in Upper Germany. Although they are not attested until 145/6, the type of fort which they occupied had first been constructed at the beginning of the century. However, even if the soldiers had been trans-ferred from Britain during Trajan's reign, it is not known whether they were forcibly drafted into the army, perhaps after warfare on the northern frontier, and sent abroad or simply recruited in the normal manner.

Loca

It has long been thought that a fifth-century document known as the *Ravenna Cosmography* records evidence for the duties of the soldiers based in the outpost forts. This document lists places in Britain (**91**). One particular section in the sector north of Hadrian's Wall is headed *diversa loca* (various places): *Maponi, Mixa, Panovius, Minox, Taba, Manavi, Segloes, Daunoni.*

Ian Richmond, in an influential overview of the northern frontier, pointed to a reference in Cassius Dio's *History of Rome* describing the establishment of *loca* (meeting-places) north of the Danube at the end of the Marcommanic Wars of Marcus Aurelius (about 180) and suggested that this section of the *Ravenna Cosmography* has preserved reference to the same arrangement on the British frontier. The meeting-places related to the known tribes: *Segloes = Selgovae, Daunoni = Damnonii*; or to places such as *Maponi = locus Maponi* (Bewcastle); while *Taba* is presumably the Tay. This suggestion receives some support from the use of the term *loca* by Ammianus Marcellinus to describe the places attacked by the Scots and the Picts near the frontier.

Richmond's hypothesis was challenged by Rivet and Smith in *The Place-Names of Roman Britain* who argued that these are not meeting-places, 'but a collection of odd names', including tribal and place-names, lumped together under the one heading. As a result it is difficult to know the value of this evidence. Perhaps the *Ravenna Cosmography* merely demonstrates that in the fifth century Roman records retained knowledge of tribes and places then well beyond the frontier of the empire.

90 *A sculpture of the goddess Brigantia dedicated by Amandus, architect-engineer, and found at Birrens. This may indicate that the tribal territory stretched into Annandale.*

91 *North Britain in the third–fourth centuries. Carpow and Cramond were both probably only occupied in the early third century. The possible loca listed in the* Ravenna Cosmography *are indicated by stars.*

Scouts

There is evidence that the Roman army did keep the area north of Hadrian's Wall under surveillance. Ammianus Marcellinus, in describing the invasion of 367, stated that:

during these outstanding events the *areani*, who had gradually become corrupt, were removed by him from their positions. This was an organization founded in early times... It

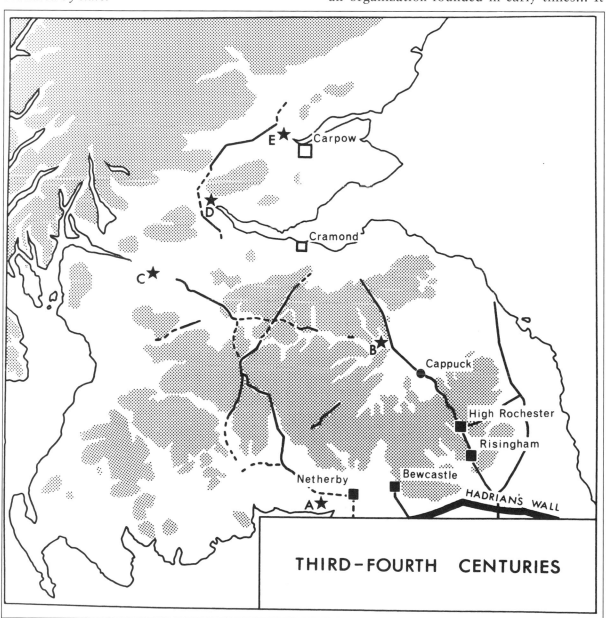

was clearly proved against them that they had been bribed with quantities of plunder, or promises of it, to reveal to the enemy from time to time what was happening on our side. Their official duty was to range backwards and forwards over long distances with information for our generals about disturbances among the neighbouring nations.

This is a classic description of scouts and their duties. In this case, they had betrayed their own masters. It is unfortunate that we do not know when this scouting system was established, though it had clearly been in existence for some considerable time: Richmond suggested that it formed part of the arrangements made by Caracalla in 211. That would certainly be consistent with Rome's views on the necessity of maintaining surveillance over the States beyond her frontiers.

Diplomacy

Rome never relied upon military force alone to obtain her aims. There is plentiful evidence from frontiers other than Britain to show that diplomacy was used when and where she did not wish to engage her armies. This might take various forms. Rome usually tried to ensure that the kings of neighbouring States were friendly disposed towards her. Military or financial support to one faction within the State might achieve this. Rome often sheltered disaffected kings or nobles who might be returned to power. Agricola had his Irish princeling to hand in 81 and such a person might have been left in control, with or without Roman support, following Roman intervention in Ireland, if such action had materialized.

Sir Ian Richmond suggested that Rome took significant new protective measures beyond her northern borders in the late fourth century (92). He argued that the Romans replaced the scouting arrangments by a network of buffer States, essentially returning to the client arrangements of earlier days. Richmond based his argument on the genealogies of the early kings of Strathclyde and Manau Gododdin. These early kings had Latin names and one was named Patern Pesrut, Patern of the Red Cloak, an epithet which was taken to imply investment by the Roman imperial authorities.

Other scholars, however, have pointed out the fallacy of the buffer-State theory. Kenneth Jackson emphasized that the genealogies may not be reliable for this period, the fourth century, while the use of Latin names may only bear witness to Roman prestige or, as John Mann has suggested, the adoption of Christianity. Finally, Patern may not be 'of the Red Cloak', but rather 'the Red Shirt'. Red is, in fact, one of the commoner dyes at Vindolanda, whereas the appropriate colour was purple when barbarian kings were invested by Rome.

The kingdoms of Strathclyde and Manau Gododdin certainly existed, but rather than newly created by Rome, it may be that we should see them as the direct descendants of the pre-Roman Iron Age tribes. The Gododdin retained the name of the Votadini, though now apparently restricted to the Forth basin, while Strathclyde's territory seems to have closely matched that of the earlier Damnonii.

It is not impossible that these States were converted to Christianity in the fourth century. Certainly when Ninian was sent from Carlisle to Whithorn, traditionally about 400, he went to a pre-existing community. At about the same time, Patrick, also perhaps from the Carlisle area, wrote admonishing the Christian Coroticus, King of Strathclyde.

Treaties

Relations between Rome and her neighbours were frequently governed by treaties. In 197, we are informed by Cassius Dio, 'the Caledonians instead of honouring their promises had prepared to defend the Maeatae'. The clear implication is that the Caledonians had a treaty with Rome. These Caledonians were presumably the descendants of the opponents of Agricola.

92 *The States of north Britain in the late fourth century.*

The Maeatae appear now for the first time, but we do not hear of them again after the Severan period. They are described as living 'by the wall which divides the island into two halves, and the Caledonians beyond them', but which Wall is not stated. Two place-names near Stirling may help here. Above the campus of Stirling University sits Dumyat, the hill of the Maeatae. Some distance to the south-west is Myot Hill. This suggests that the Wall was the Antonine Wall, even though we believe that it had been abandoned by this time. How far the Maeatae extended beyond these two place-names is not known. It is likely that Dumyat and Myot Hill

lay on the edge of the territory of the Maeatae and were so named by their neighbours.

There was a treaty therefore between the Romans, whose main frontier installations lay on Hadrian's Wall, and Caledonians 200km (120 miles) to the north, and possibly also with the Maeatae in between. We know nothing about the treaties, except that they were presumably non-aggression pacts and that they were broken by the Caledonians and Maeatae. Warfare appears to have continued in the north until reaching a climax with the invasions of Septimius Severus and Caracalla. After his father's death, Caracalla made treaties with the enemy when evacuating their territory.

In spite of the Romans' troubled relations with the Picts, there was a treaty between the

111

two States, for Ammianus Marcellinus recorded that in 360 the Scots and Picts disrupted the agreed peace. It is not impossible that there were treaties between Rome and her northern neighbours throughout most of our period.

Subsidies

Other forms of diplomatic contact existed. In 197 the Romans 'had to buy peace from the Maeatae for a considerable sum, recovering a few captives'. The existence of coin hoards in Scotland dating to the late second and early third centuries suggests that the Romans 'purchased' peace again through the payment of subsidies or bribes (it depends on one's point of view) to the northern tribes.

These coin hoards include one from Rumbling Bridge between the Forth and the Tay which ends with a coin of 184. The 100 coins in the hoard were clearly carefully chosen for it includes one coin for each of the years 180 to 184. Four hoards ending with coins of Severus are known from Scotland. A further hoard, from Falkirk, beside the Antonine Wall, ends in 235 (**colour plate 11**). Fourth-century hoards are also known, from as far north as Fort Augustus in the Great Glen, the north-east coast at Covesea Cave, and the far south-west of Scotland. It is possible that all of these hoards reflect subsidies paid by the Romans to their northern neighbours.

Subsidies did not have to be paid in cash (**colour plate 12**). Fine glass vessels found in Aberdeenshire and in Orkney may also have been diplomatic gifts given by Rome to northern chiefs or kings (**93**). An unusual find at the Broch of Gurness in Orkney was a fragment from an amphora dating to the 100 years between the mid-first century BC and the mid-first century AD. Andrew Fitzpatrick has linked this to the recorded submission of the Orkney islands to Claudius in 43. We might see here the remnant of a diplomatic gift, or, as Fitzpatrick prefers, a hint at alliances between the Iron Age tribes. Generally, the hoards and

93 *A glass vessel found at Turriff in Aberdeenshire.*

glass vessels have been stray finds, and thus little can be said about their context. One site is distinctive, however, in the range of high-quality goods found there, Traprain Law.

Traprain Law

Traprain Law in Lothian had been occupied for many centuries before the Romans arrived (**colour plate 13**). Artefacts of the Neolithic period may indicate human activity there over 3000 years before the Romans. Occupation continued, though not necessarily continuously, into the fifth century AD. Traprain Law appears to have been in use at the time of Agricola's

94 *A stone carved with the letters* ABCD *found at Traprain Law.*

could have been a subsidy or a diplomatic gift paid to the local chief or king by the Romans. The way in which the treasure was cut up suggests that it was not going to be used as tableware, but that does not in itself rule out its use as payment to a king. The presence of some fine late Roman glass at Traprain may also point to friendly diplomatic relations between Rome and the Votadini.

It was the scale and nature of the Roman material on Traprain Law and the fact that the hilltop town continued in occupation throughout the Roman period which first led to the suggestion that the people of this site and their tribe enjoyed a special relationship with Rome, perhaps being a client State. Sometimes the argument is supported by the contention that there were no Roman forts in the territory of the tribe during those periods when southern Scotland lay within the province. There were, however, military posts, including a fort at *Bremenium,* High Rochester, listed by Ptolemy, within Votadinian territory. Furthermore, it was not necessary for the Romans to physically occupy territory in order to control its occupants: they could exercise their will by threat of force.

There have been two recent attempts to re-evaluate the relationship between Rome and Traprain Law. Analysis of the coins and other

advance. It is the only hill-fort which can be shown to have continued in occupation during the Roman period, though small amounts of third- and fourth-century pottery have been found within the defences of the fort on Eildon Hill North, and it was a major settlement extending to over 16ha (40 acres).

Traprain Law boasts the largest assemblage of Roman artefacts found at a civilian site. These include brooches, pottery, a stone marked with the letters ABCD, and, the famous Traprain Treasure (**94, 95, colour plate 14**). This dates to about 400 and contains fragments of fifty metal objects. Nearly all the objects have been cut or broken up in antiquity. The hoard remains enigmatic. It may have been loot gathered by the inhabitants of Traprain Law in raids on the empire. Alternatively, the treasure

95 *Moulds for dress-fasteners found at Traprain Law.*

96 *Map of Roman artefacts dating to the later third and fourth centuries found in Scotland. The cluster of finds in the Glasgow area suggests that some items may be modern losses.*

artefacts has not only emphasized their uniqueness in a Scottish context, but compared them to assemblages from temples leading to the suggestion that the artefacts were deposited in a native shrine on the hill.

The suggestion that Traprain Law was the site of a temple and not a town cannot be dismissed out of hand. Such religious centres did exist at the time in both the Celtic and the Roman worlds. Nor need Traprain Law be unique. Roman artefacts in a possible religious site at Covesea Cave on the Moray coast may have been offerings to the gods.

While the nature of the contact between Rome and the inhabitants of Traprain Law may be uncertain, what cannot be denied is that there was contact and that that contact continued over several centuries.

Trade

It is very difficult to make much of the other finds from beyond the frontier (**96**). Most have been found along the coast which perhaps indicates the main lines of communication. They have been found as far west as the Western Isles and as far north as Shetland: the few Roman artefacts found in Norway may have travelled there via Scotland. Tacitus recorded that the ports and harbours of

Ireland were tolerably well known by Agricola's day from merchants who traded there and this is supported by Ptolemy who demonstrated greater knowledge of the interior of Ireland than northern Scotland.

Traders, explorers, refugees, missionaries, raiders or even returning Roman soldiers, all might have accounted for the appearance of Roman artefacts beyond the imperial frontier. A burial in the Roman manner discovered on the shores of Luce Bay in the south-west may have been that of a Roman trader or sailor. It might seem strange to suggest that some objects drifted north through the action of Roman soldiers returning home. Certainly while there is no evidence for Caledonians entering the Roman army, other foreigners, such as Germans, are known to have been recruited so it is clearly a possibility. In fact, there is a record of a Caledonian from Colchester. Another Caledonian export was the bear which was sent to Rome, presumably by Agricola, to take part in the opening festivities at the Colosseum in 80.

The impact of the frontier

In the 1950s Eric Birley argued that 'Hadrian's Wall was primarily devised as a boundary within which Romanization was to be developed, and the natural corollary was the growth of farms and villages and towns, settled agriculture and the arts of peace'; in fact, 'peace could be maintained by an ambitious policy of economic development along the frontiers of the empire, backed up by the intelligent deployment' of the army. Such a view would imply that differences would grow up between the social structures and settlement patterns on either side of the Wall. One major difference, of course, was the growth of villages and towns along the Wall and elsewhere within the province. More recently aerial photography has led to another distinction being proposed.

Survey in the Solway basin has led to the suggestion that sites were different north and south of Hadrian's Wall. South of the Solway, most settlements can be seen to have had only one ditch, and were elliptical, though there were some sub-rectangular sites. To the north, the settlement density was less, there were very few sub-rectangular sites, while more of the elliptical enclosures were protected by two or more ditches. Field systems are known south of the Solway, but hardly at all to the north.

East of the Pennines, differences in the distribution of rectilinear and curvilinear settlements have been recognized but have been ascribed to the topography: the former are generally found on the plain, the latter on the hills. However, Marijke van der Veen has suggested that the distinctions she has recognized between the small-scale farming regime growing mainly emmer wheat and barley in northern Northumberland and the larger-scale, more extensive regime growing improved spelt wheat and barley in the Tees lowlands, may be indicative of deep-rooted differences between the two areas.

Rome and the Picts: cause and effect?

The impact of the Romans on the native people of north Britain has already been discussed. The arrival of these new masters must have had a deep psychological effect not only upon those conquered, but also on those who remained beyond the empire. The native States alone were no match for Rome and from the earliest days combined to oppose this new force in the north. Tacitus described this process at the battle of Mons Graupius. It is presumably significant therefore that, as the years progress, we see a gradual coalescence of the tribes beyond the empire. Twelve were listed by Ptolemy in the second century, though presumably representing the situation at the time of Agricola (see **28**). At the end of the second century only the Caledonians and Maeatae are mentioned, and Dio states that 'the names of the others have been included in these' (see **89**). A century later, in 297, we first hear of the Picts (**97**). A panegyric of the

97 *Picts, mounted and on foot, depicted on the Aberlemno churchyard symbol stone.*

Emperor Constantine delivered in 310 refers to 'the Caledonians and other Picts', demonstrating their ancestry. Divisions within the Picts are still noted by Roman writers. The *Verona List* of 314 mentions the Scoti, Picti and Caledonii; Ammianus Marcellinus states that the Picts were divided into two tribes, the Dicalydonae and the Verturiones.

This gradual amalgamation of the separate tribes into a single nation may owe something to Rome. The only way which the northern people could hope to oppose the Roman army successfully was through the creation of a unified and therefore larger State. Exactly the same process can be seen on the Continent, where the smaller nations were superceded by larger groupings who were able to overcome the frontier armies and conquer the western empire in the fifth century. Here, therefore, is perhaps the greatest gift Rome was able to give to her northern neighbours: the impetus to unify. In view of the threats from other quarters which the Picts soon had to face (see Sally Foster's *Picts, Gaels and Scots* in this series), this may not have been a negligible gift.

117

Monuments and museums to visit

The surviving monuments are all earthworks except where stated. All monuments are accessible to the public, though some are on private land: those marked by an * are in the care of Historic Scotland. Visitors should always follow the Country Code. Most monuments appear on the maps 38 and 88.

Antonine Wall

The ditch is visible intermittently from Callendar Park, Falkirk to Twechar; the best stretch of ditch is at *Watling Lodge, Falkirk (see 48); the best surviving length of rampart is at *Rough Castle, Bonnybridge, where there are also the best fort and annexe earthworks (see colour plate 8); the stone base is visible in Hillfoot Cemetery, Bearsden; the military way is visible at *Seabegs Wood and at *Rough Castle where there are visible quarry pits; fort buildings may be seen at *Bar Hill (headquarters and bath-house) and *Bearsden (bath-house and latrine: see colour plates 9 and 10); a fortlet lies at Kinneil, Bo'ness, with the finds in the adjacent museum; 'expansions' can be seen at *Rough Castle and on the west side of *Croy Hill. The 10km (6 miles) from Castlecary to Twechar, over Croy Hill (see 46) and Bar Hill, forms a good walk with the ditch visible for most of the route.

Ardoch, Braco, Perthshire (NN 840100)

The fort earthworks are among the best preserved anywhere in the empire (see 1). Beyond the second-century rampart are five ditches to east and north; an earlier second-century rampart lies embedded in the north defences. Also surviving are parts of the annexe and three camps. The rampart of one *camp was slighted when its successor was built.

Birrens, Middlebie, Dumfries and Galloway (NY 218752)

The rampart of this second-century fort is protected by six ditches to the north.

Bothwellhaugh, Strathclyde Country Park, Hamilton (NS 730577)

Second-century bath-house in Strathclyde Country Park.

Burnswark, Middlebie, Dumfries and Galloway (NY 185787)

There survive here the earthworks of an Iron Age hill-fort and, on each side, a Roman camp: the south camp overlay a fortlet.

Castle Greg (NT 050592)

The rampart and ditch of a fortlet, probably dating to the first century.

Cramond, Edinburgh (NT 189769)

Several buildings in the north part of this second-century fort have been marked out. *Eagle Rock, across the River Almond, is believed to be a Roman carving.

*Dere Street, Soutra (NT 464567)
 A well-preserved stretch of road, with quarry pits to the side (see **colour plate 5**).

Dumfries Museum
Material from south-west Scotland.

Dundee, McManus Art Gallery and Museum
The finds from Carpow and the area.

Durisdeer, Dumfries and Galloway
(NS 902048)
The rampart and ditch of a second-century fortlet.

Edinburgh, Huntly House Museum
Finds from Cramond.

Edinburgh, National Museum of Antiquities
The core of the collection is the material from the 1905–10 excavations at Newstead. Other material from Scotland.

Gask Ridge, Perthshire
The earthworks of several towers are visible, including *Ardunie (NN 946187) and *Muir o'Fauld (NN 981189).

Glasgow, Art Gallery and Museum, Kelvingrove
Finds from the west of Scotland.

Glasgow, Hunterian Museum
Material from the Antonine Wall and west of Scotland, including most of the distance slabs.

Inchtuthil, Meikleour (NO 125396)
Parts of the east, west and south defences of the fortress are visible.

*Jedburgh Abbey
Roman inscription in site museum.

Kirkintilloch Museum
Local material.

Lyne (NT 187405)
The ramparts of this second-century fort survive together with the outer ditch on two sides.

Melrose
Some finds from Newstead: there are also some artefacts at the *abbey.

Pennymuir, Towford (NT 754140)
Almost the complete circuit of the defences of this camp and five of its six gates are visible, with another camp in one corner.

Further reading

Primary sources

The best compilations of original sources are:

Dobson, B. and Maxfield V.A. (eds) *Inscriptions from Roman Britain*, London Association of Classical Teachers (LACTOR 4), 1995.

Mann, J.C. and Penman, R.G. (eds) *Literary Sources for Roman Britain*, London Association of Classical Teachers (LACTOR 11), 1985.

Rivet, A.L.F. and Smith, C. *The Place-Names of Roman Britain*, London, 1979.

These do not include:

Caesar, *The Gallic War*. There is a Penguin translation.

Tacitus, *Agricola*. There is a translation by Penguin, and a commentary by R.M. Ogilvie and I.A. Richmond, *de vita Agricola*, Oxford, 1965.

Tacitus, *Annals*. Penguin translation.

For inscriptions and documents see:

Roman Inscriptions of Britain, vol. I; vol. II fascicules 1–8, Oxford 1965–95.

Bowman, A.K. and Thomas, J.K. *The Vindolanda Writing Tablets (Tabula Vindolandenses II)*, London, 1994.

Keppie, L.J.F. 'Roman Inscriptions from Scotland: additions and corrections to RIB I', *Proceedings of the Society of Antiquaries of Scotland* 113 (1983), 391–404.

Secondary sources

Barrett, J., Fitzpatrick, A. and Macinnes, Lesley (eds) *Barbarians and Romans in North-West Europe*, Oxford, 1989 (= BAR IS 471).

Birley, E. *Roman Britain and the Roman Army*, Kendal, 1961.

Breeze, D.J. *The Northern Frontiers of Roman Britain*, London, 1982.

Breeze, D.J. and Dobson, B. *Hadrian's Wall*, 3rd edn, London, 1987.

Breeze, D.J. and Dobson, B. *Roman Officers and Frontiers*, Stuttgart, 1993.

Davies, R.W. *Service in the Roman Army*, ed. David Breeze and Valerie Maxfield, Edinburgh, 1989.

Hanson, W.S. *Agricola and the Conquest of the North*, London, 1991.

Hanson, W.S. and Maxwell, G.S. *Rome's North-west Frontier: the Antonine Wall*, Edinburgh, 1986.

Keppie, L. 'The Antonine Wall 1960–1980', *Britannia* 13 (1982), 91–111.

Keppie, L. *Scotland's Roman Remains*, Edinburgh, 1986.

Macinnes, L. 'Brochs and the Roman Occupation of Lowland Scotland', *Proceedings of the Society of Antiquaries of Scotland* 114 (1984), 235–49.

Maxwell, G.S. *The Romans in Scotland*, Edinburgh, 1989.

Maxwell, G.S. *A Battle Lost: Romans and Caledonians at Mons Graupius*, Edinburgh, 1990.

Millar, F. 'Emperors, Frontiers and Foreign Relations, 31 BC to AD 378', *Britannia* 13 (1982), 1–23.

Robertson, A.S. 'The Romans in North Britain: the coin evidence', in Temporini, H. and Haase, W. (eds) *Aufstieg und Niedergang des Römischen Welt*, II, 3, Berlin and New York, 1975, 364–426.

Robertson, A.S. *The Antonine Wall*, rev. edn by Keppie, L.J.F., Glasgow, 1990.

Whittaker, C.R. *Frontiers of the Roman Empire*, Cambridge, 1994.

Index

(Page numbers in **bold** refer to illustrations)

Aberlemno, churchyard stone **116**
administration and government, in frontier
 zone 83
aerial photographs 14, 16, 26–7, 28, 115
Agricola, Julius 13, 16–17, 18, 19, 35, 100–1
 battle of Mons Graupius 16, 17, 47–8, 91, 97
 biography by Tacitus (*Agricola*) 16, 20, 35, 47
 and the Caledonians 45–8
 coin evidence 26
 conquest of the north 17, 20, 33–43
 and garrisons 17, 58, 59, 60
 as governor 11, 16, 33, 35, 61
 invasion of southern Scotland 44–5
 and the Irish prince 30, 110
 and the Ordovices 16–17, 30, 33, 35
 takes hostages 45, 53
 taxation 84
altars 71, 87, 95
 at Birrens 74, 81–2, **89**
 at Castlecary 23, **23**, 82, 87, 95
 at Corbridge 103
Ambleside
 sling bullets 80
 tombstone 83, 103–4
amphitheatres 79
amphorae **62**, 112
animal bones 84–5
annexes *see* forts
Antonine Wall 12, 15, **15**, 16, 17, 18, 20, 24, 58, 63–9, **65**,
 92, 107, 111, 119, **colour plate 7**
 coins 26, 58, 95
 expansions 15, 67, **68**
 forts and fortlets 64, **64**, 66–8, **68**, 69
 inscriptions 22, 29, 68–9
 labour camps and camps 14, 69
 pits 66
 turf construction 24, 64, **65**
 withdrawal from 94–5
Apollinaris, Julius 75
Apollo Grannus 12
Arague, Asia Minor 86
Ardestie, settlement **colour plate 16**
Ardoch, fort and camp 13, 14, **14**, 25, **25**, 57, 119
army 27, 29, 38–40
 auxiliary units 31, 38, 39, 42, **44**, **48**, 53, 57, 68, **colour plate 4**
 cavalry 39, 42, **49**, 70, 74, 97
 centuries 38
 centurions 73, 74, 80
 cohorts 38
 commanding officer 12, 71, 76–7

conscription 89, 90
decurions 39, 73, 74
equipment and logistics 12, 40–2, **40**, **41**
food and food supplies 12, **24**, 40–2, **41**, 77–8, **77**, **78**,
 84–5, 90, 100
German soldiers 12, 74, 115
immunes 74
junior tribunes 39
legate 38
legions and legionaries **31**, 38, 39, **39**, 42, 53, 68, 80,
 colour plate 3
life in the fort 26, 75–6
life outside the fort 82–3
officers and men 38–9, 73–5, **73**
pay 74, 80
prefects 38–9, 74
relations with local people 87–9
religion 80–2
sentry duty 75
size of 106
soldiers 12, 74–5
supplies 26, 84–6, 100
surveyors 42, 43
taxation and customs duties collected by 83–4
tents 40, 43, **43**, **85**
training 15, 78–80
tribune 74
tribunus laticlavius 38
artefacts 26, 27, **27**, 87–9, 112–15, **114**
 see also coins; pottery
Arthur's O'on **51**, 52
Auchendavy, altars 82
Augustus, Emperor 38, 93–4, 99
Aurelius, Marcus 17, 24, 96

Balmuildy
 Antonine Wall 64
 fort 66
 inscriptions 66–7
 statue of Mars **81**
Bar Hill, fort 15, **72**
 bath-house **72**, 119
 burial near 12
 headquarters building **75**, 119
 hearths 86
 pottery kiln 87
Barburgh Mill, fortlet **82**
Barochan 59
Batavians 31, 84
bath-houses 15, **72**, 73, 76, 119, **colour plate 9**
 Fortuna 81, **81**

beacon–platforms, possible 15, 67, **68**
Bearsden
  analysis of sewage 77, 78
  bath–house and latrine 15, 119, **colour plates 9 & 10**
  food 85
  fort 55, **55**
  gaming board **82**
  head of a goddess **81**
  Sarrius, potter 87
  withdrawal **95**
Bennachie, hill 47
Benwell, inscription 24
Bertha, fort 57, 58
Bewcastle
  as *Maponi* 107
  station 105, 107
Birdoswald
  fort 63
  sling bullets 80
Birrens 14, 25
  altar to German gods 74, 81–2, **89**
  Brigantia, sculpture of 82, **108**
  fort 73, 107
  rampart and ditches 119
  rebuilding 94
  sling bullets 80
  station 107
  stone buildings 25
Bochastle, fort 56
Bolanus, Vettius, governor 19, 34
Bothwellhaugh, bath–house 119
Boudica 19, 31
Bremenium see High Rochester
Bridgeness, distance–slab **32, 49**
Brigantes 12, 19, 20, 31, 33, 34, 61, 94, 103, 107
Britannica, as title 51
Britannicus, as title 22, 52
Brittones 107
Broch of Gurness, amphora 112
brochs 88–9, 90, **colour plate 15**
brooches **27**
Broxmouth, defences 90
Buchlyvie broch 88
building materials *see* Antonine Wall; stone structures;
  timber structures
burials 87, **89**, 115
Burnswark 25
  camps 79–80, **79**, 119
  hill–fort 90, 119
  sling bullets 80, **80**
  training area 15, **79**

Cadder, timber buildings 86
Caesar, Julius 11, 30, 36, 40–1, 53, 102
Caledonian mountains 97–9
Caledonians 11, 17, 20, 30, 35, 36, 45–7, 57, 97, 115, 117
  at Mons Graupius 47–8, 50, 51, 91
  invasions 103–4
  in the Roman army 115
  treaties with the Romans 17, 110, 111
  war trumpet **colour plate 1**
Caligula 30–1
Camelon
  burial cist 87
  fort 25, 53, 56, 58
camps (marching–camps; temporary) 13–14, **14**, 27, 42, **42**,
  43, **44**, 45–7, **46**, 58, 69, 79–80, **79**
  see also labour camps
Cappadocia 12, 85, 106
Cappuck 25

Caracalla 11, 13, 18, 20, 22, 51, 96, 102, 110, 111
  face–jar **96**
Cardean, fort 57
Carlisle
  fort 34, 36, 92
  fort west of 61
  writing tablets 24
carpenters and tools **54, 55**
Carpow
  fortress 14, 22, 26, 57, 85, 96
  inscription 14, 29, 96, **96**
Carrawburgh, fort 63
Carriden
  dedication to Jupiter 83
  fields 86
Cartimandua 33, 34, 94
Carvoran
  fort 63
  rations 78
Castle Greg, fortlet 119
Castlecary
  fort 25, 66, 67
  inscription on altar (shrine to Mercury) 23, **23**, 82, 87, 95
  pottery 92
Castledykes, fort 53, 93
Cerialis, Petillius 33, 34, 36, 92
Charax, Claudius 12, 32
Chesters, inscription 24
Chlorus, Constantius 18, 105
Christianity 110
civil settlements 26, 86–7
civitates 83, **104**
Claudius, Emperor 11, 12, 30, 31, 34, 36, 52, 99, 102, 112
cohors I Baetasiorum 51
cohors I Cugernorum 51, 103
cohors I Hispanorum 51
cohors II Austurum 103
cohors II Tungrorum 74
cohors XX Palmyrenorum 75, 76, 82
coin hoards 112
coins 22, 26, 29, 52, 84
  from the Antonine Wall 26, 58, 95
  with Britannia **17**, 22, 94, **95**
  of Domitian 36
  evidence for abandonment of forts 91
  at Inchtuthil 55
  at Old Kilpatrick 26, 95
  of Pius **17**
  of Severus **18**, 22
  from Traprain Law 113
Commodus, Emperor 17, 24, 96
Constans 11, 18, 105
Constantine the Great, Emperor 11, 18, 105, 106, 117,
  colour plate 2
Corbridge
  altar 103
  as Coria 76, 80
  fort 94
  fort east of 61
  inscription 22, **23**, 29, 103
  sling bullets 80
Coria, as place–name 44
Coria (Corbridge) 76, 80
Corionototae 103
Covesea Cave
  artefacts 114
  coin hoard 112
Cramond
  dedication to Jupiter **81**
  fort 12, 57, 85, 119

pottery 96
Crawford 94
Croy Hill
    Antonine Wall 64, **65**, 119
    fields 86
    tombstone sculpture **28**

Dalginross, fort 56
Dalswinton, fort 53, 70, 92, 93
Damnonii 44, 107, 110
Demetrius 36, 38
Dere Street 22, 61, 119
Digest of Roman Law 82
Dio, Cassius, historian 16, 17, 18, 20, 22, 24, 29, 50, 57, 96, 107, 115
Diocletian 11, 105, 106
diplomacy 110
diplomas 23–4
diplomatic gifts 112, 113
distance-slabs **32**, **49**, 68–9, **69**, 95
Dolichenus, god 12
Domitian 20, 35, 86, 91, 100–1, 102
    coin **36**
Doune, fort 57
Dowalton, cooking pot (*patera*) **40**
Drumquhassle, fort 56
Dumfries, museum 120
Dumyat 111
Dundee, museum 14, 120
Duntocher, fort **15**
Dura Europos 75, 76, 80–1, 82
Durisdeer, fortlet 120, **colour plate 6**
Durno, camp 47

Eagle Rock, carving 119
Edinburgh
    Castle, brooches **27**
    museums 120
Edin's Hall, broch **colour plate 15**
Egypt 85
Eildon Hill North, fort 90, 113
Elginhaugh, fort **71**, 92
emperors 11, 22, 100–2
enclosures 67
excavation and survey, as sources 24–7

face masks 79, **79**
Falkirk, coin hoard 112, **colour plate 11**
farming and farmsteads 90, **90**, 115
    tribal economy 99
Fendoch, fort 56
field armies 39–40, 106
fields and field systems 86, 115
Firmus, Cocceius, altars erected by 82
Flavian period (dynasty) 20, 29, **56**, 92, **93**
fleet 13, 38, 39, 40, 45
food and food supplies 12, **24**, 77–8, **77**, **78**, 84–5, 90, 100
Fort Augustus, coin hoard 112
fortlets (outposts) 15, 16, 53, 54, 59–60, 61, **64**, 67, 68, **68**, 82, 107
    see also Hadrian's Wall, milecastles
fortresses 13, 14
    amphitheatres 79
    size 73
    see also Carpow; Inchtuthil
forts 14–15, 22, 25, 53–4, 55–7, 70–3, 107
    altars 82
    annexes 14, 67, 73
    on Antonine Wall 64, **64**, 66–8, **68**
    assembly hall (*basilica*) 70

bath–houses 15, **72**, 73, 76, **colour plate 9**
building work 54–5, **54**, **55**
and civil settlements 86–7
commanding officer's house (*praetorium*) 70, 71, **72**
distances between 26–7, 53
granaries (*horreum*) 70, **71**, **72**, 73, 85
and Hadrian's Wall 61, 62, 63, 67
Hanoverian 98–9, **98**
headquarters building (*principia*) 70, **71**, **72**, 75, **75**, 82
hearths and ovens 78
latrines 70, 73
life in 75–6
ramparts 42
shrine (*aedes*) 70–1
sizes 57
and supplies 84
withdrawal and abandonment 91–4, **93**, **101**
    see also fortlets; fortresses
Frissii 84
frontier system (zone) 59–61, 106–7
Frontinus, Julius 16–17, 33
gaming board **82**
Gask Ridge 25, 59, **59**, 120
    tower 15, **60**
Gaul 12, 30, 40, 42
    soldiers from 74
geography of Britain 20–1, **21**, 36, **37**, 38
Germany 12, 39, 55, 60, 107
    soldiers from 12, 74, 115
Geta 11, 22
Glasgow, museums 120
Glasgow Archaeological Society 24, 64
glass 112, **112**, 113
Glenlochar, fort 53, 92, 93
Gododdin 110
gods and goddesses 12, 81–2, 87
governors of Britain 11–12, 33, 106
grain 78, 84, 85
granaries 70, **71**, **72**, 85, 86, **100**
Greatchesters, fort 63

Hadrian, Emperor 11, 17, 61, 63, 79, 94, 101, 102
Hadrian's Wall 11, 17, 20, 61–3, **61**, **62**, **63**, 92, 94, 106, 107, 111, 115
    forts 61, 62, 63, 67, 69, 105
    inscriptions 18, 24, 29
    milecastles 61, 62, 63, 95
    monument 52
    recommissioned 29, 94, 95
    roads and path 66
    Vallum 62–3, **63**, 67, 95
Hanoverian forts and roads 98–9, **98**
Hawkshaw, carved head **52**, 82
Helmsdale, bowls **colour plate 12**
Herodian 18, 20, 29, 57, 97
High Rochester
    as *Bremenium* 44, 113
    fort **105**, 107
Highland Line forts 56, 57
hill-forts 15, 90, 113
Horsley, John, *Britannia Romana* 29
Hutcheson Hill, distance-slab **69**

Iceni 31
Inchtuthil
    fortress 14, 25, 55, 57, **58**, 60, 120
    labour camps **28**, 55
    abandonment 91
    nails 91–2, **91**
industry 87

Ingliston milestone **69**
inscriptions 22–4, 26, 54, 73, 103, 106, 107
    on Antonine Wall distance-slabs 22, 29, 68–9
    at Balmuildy 66–7
    at Carpow 14, 29, 96, **96**
    at Castlecary 23, **23**, 95
    at Corbridge 22, **23**, 29, 103
    at Inveresk 86–7
    at Kirksteads 103
    at Rough Castle 25
invasion of Britain 30–3
Inveravon, platform 67
Inveresk
    fort and civil settlement 86, 87
    inscriptions 86–7
Ireland 17, 115
Italy 12

Jedburgh
    Abbey 120
    outpost fort and inscriptions 107
Josephus, writer 21, 40, 42
Judaea 85
Julian, Emperor 42

Kaimes Castle, fortlet 25, 59–60
Kirkintilloch, museum 120
Kirksteads, inscription 103

labour camps 14, **28**, 55
leather 40, 84
Leckie broch 88
legate 73
legio II Adiutrix 92
legio II Augusta 12, **23**, 31, **32**, 68, 69
legio IX 39, 43, 45
legio IX Hispana 31, 35
legio VI Victrix **23**, 51, 68, 103
legio XIV 31
legio XX Valeria Victrix 31, **31**, 36, **55**, 68, **69**
legions *see* army
literary sources 16–22, 54
loca 107, **109**
Loudon Hill 92
Luce Bay, burial 115
Lucilla, Empress, coin of 26
Lyne, fort 25, 120

Maeatae 17, 30, 35, 51, 103, 104, 110, 111, 112, 115
Maeshowe, chambered tomb 100
Manau Gododdin 110
Maponi see Bewcastle
maps 38
Marcellinus, Ammianus 20, 105, 107, 109–10, 112, 117
Marcellus, Ulpius 17, 18
    coin 22
    diploma 24
marching–camps *see* camps
Maximus, Magnus 105–6
medicines 78
Melrose 120
merchants 12, 87
milecastles *see* Hadrian's Wall
milestone, at Ingliston **69**
military treatises 21–2
Military Way (road) 15, 66
Milsington, statue leg 82
Milton, fort 53, 92, 93
Mollins, fort 59
Mons Graupius, battle of 16, 17, 35, 36, 39, 45, 47–51, 91,

97, 115
monuments 13–16
Mousa, broch 99
Mumrills
    fort 66
    tombstone of Nectovelius 74, **74**
Myot Hill 111

Nectovelius, tombstone of 74, **74**
Nepos, Platorius 24
Netherby, station 105, 107
Newstead, fort 25–6, 53, 73, 92, 93, 94
    amphitheatre 79
    animal bone 84
    carpenters' tools **55**
    cart wheel **86**
    commanding officer 77
    cremation urn **89**
    face masks 79, **79**
    phalerae **50**
    querns and cooking pots 77
    tent peg and mallet **43**
    as *Trimontium* 44
    turf cutter 40, **43**
    water flask **40**
    writing tablets 24
Ninian 110
Noricum 12
Norway 114
Notitia Dignitatum 106
Novantae 44

Oakwood, fort 92
officers *see* army
Old Kilpatrick, fort 66
    coin 26, 95
Orcades, kingdom of the 103
Ordovices 16–17, 30, 33, 35
Orkney islands 16, 36, 45, **99**
    glass vessels 112
outpost forts *see* fortlets

Parthia (Persia) 30, 42, 106
patera (cooking pot) **40**
Patern Pesrut, king 110
Patrick (St) 110
Pausanius 19, 20, 103
Pennymuir, temporary camp **42**, 120
Persia *see* Parthia
phalerae (medals) **50**, 51
Picts 18–19, 103, 105–6, 111–12, 115, **116**, 117
Pius, Antoninus 12, 17, 25, 101, 102, 103
    coinage 17
    as *imperator* 22, 29, 51
    life of 16, 29, 34
Plautius, Aulus 31, 33
Pliny the Elder 34, 36
pollen analysis 41
Polybius 21, 41
population size 90
pottery 12, 26, 27, 29, 57, 58, 60, 92, 96, 113
    Antonine Wall, from expansion 67
    evidence for withdrawal 95
    Greek inscription on 77
    jars (*amphorae*) 78, 112
    made in Scotland 26, 87, **88**
    samian ware 26, 95
Priscus, Statius 12, 106
Ptolemy, *Geography* 16, 20–1, **21**, 36, 37, 44, **44**, 45, 46,
    103, 115

Raetia 12
Ravenna Cosmography 107, **109**
religion 12, 26, 80–2
Richborough, monument 52
Risingham, fort 105, 107
roads 15, 54, 61, 69
Rough Castle
    fort and annexe 15, 25, 119, **colour plate 9**
    inscription 25
    pits 66, 119
    rampart 64, 119
    road and quarry pits 15
Roy, William, surveyor 15–16, **15**, 29
Royal Commission on the Ancient and
    Historical Monuments of Scotland 16
Rumbling Bridge, coin hoards 112

Salmanes 12
Sarrius, potter 87
Scaptopara, Thrace 86
scouts 38, 109–10
Selgovae 44, 107
settlements 90, 115, **colour plate 16**
Severus, Julius 12, 97, 106
Severus, Septimius 11, 13, 16, 17, 18, 35, 36, 51, 83, 102,
    111
    Britannicus as title 52
    coins **18**, 22
    Dio as a literary source for 16, 18, 20
    food supplies 85, 100
    and the praetorian guard 12, 39
Shetland 36, 114
Shirva, sepulchral relief **89**
signal-stations or watch-towers 13, 15
slaves 73
slingers and sling bullets 80, **80**
Society of Antiquaries of Scotland 24
souterrains 84, 90
South Shields, supply base 85, 96, 100, **100**
Soutra, Roman road **colour plate 5**
Stanegate 61, 62, 63, 66
States (tribal client States) 93–4, 103, **104**, 106, 110, **111**,
    113, 115, 117
Statius, poet 19, 34
Stilicho 106
Stobi, Bulgaria 85
stone structures **25**, 54, 85, 86, 90, *and see* Hadrian's Wall
Strabo 99
Stracathro, fort 57
Strageath, fort 57
Strathclyde 110
Strathspey 57
subsidies (payment to tribes) 17, 112, 113
surveyors 42, 43, 74
Syria 85

Tacitus, Cornelius, historian 16–17, 19, 26, 29, 30, 33–4, 35,
    39, 40, 41, 45, 51, 53, 54
    as a Flavian supporter 20
    on impact of Romans on local people 89–90
    on Ireland 114–15
    on Mons Graupius 16, 17, 45, 47, 48, 115
    on soldiers' pay 80

on taxation 84
    use of *topoi* (set phrases) 19
taxation 83–4, 89, 90
temples 82, 87, **89**, 114
Tentfield Plantation **colour plate 7**
Tertullus, Minthonius, dedication to Jupiter **81**
Theodosius, Count 19, 39–40, 105
Theodosius, Emperor 20
Thule 20, 36, 45
timber structures 25, 54–5, 59, 70, 86, 90, 95
Titus, Emperor 11, 35, 102
tombstones
    of Nectovelius **74**
    see also Ambleside; Croy Hill
towers 59–61, **60**
trade 12, 114–15, **114**
training areas 15, 79–80
Trajan, Emperor 20, 94, 102
Trajan's Column 40, **44**, **48**, 54, 55
    officers and standard bearers **73**
    road building **19**
    slinger 80
Tranent, inscription on stamp 77
Traprain Law 88, 112–14, **colour plates 13 & 14**
treaties 17, 110–12
tribal boundaries 106
tribes 17–18, **21**, 24, 33, 44–5, **44**, 53, 83, 94, 102, 103, 115,
    117
    social and economic infrastructure 99–100
    south–east Britain 31, 33
    subsidies to 112
Trimontium see Newstead
turf cutter 40, **43**
Turriff, glass vessel **112**
Tweed valley, stone platform 82

underground passages *see* souterrains
Urbicus, Lollius, governor 12, 17, 22, 34, 66–7

Vallum *see* Hadrian's Wall
Verona List 117
Verus, Julius, governor 12, 95
Vespasian, Emperor 11, 33, **33**, 34, 35, 102
victory medals and monuments 51–2
villas 90
Vindolanda
    letters of commanding officers 76–7
    red dye 110
    sling bullets 80
    supply lists 85–6
    writing tablets 24, **24**, 54, 76, 78, 80, 83, 97
Votadini 44, 107, 110, 113

Wallsend, fort 63
water flask, bronze 40
Watling Lodge, Antonine Wall ditch **66**, 119
Westerwood, inscription 73
Whin Sill 106
Whithorn 110
Wilderness Plantation, fortlet and
    enclosures 67
Woden Law 15
writing tablets 24, **24**, 54, 76, 78, 80, 83

The author
David Breeze is Chief Inspector of Ancient Monuments with Historic Scotland and Visiting Professor of Archaeology at the University of Durham. He has excavated extensively in north Britain and published numerous books and articles on Roman frontiers and the Roman army.

Titles in the series:

Scotland's First Settlers
Caroline Wickham–Jones
Neolithic and Bronze Age Scotland
P.J. Ashmore
Prehistoric Orkney
Anna Ritchie
Picts, Gaels and Scots
Sally Foster
Viking Scotland
Anna Ritchie
Medieval Scotland
Peter Yeoman
Scottish Abbeys and Priories
Richard Fawcett
Fortress Scotland and the Jacobites
Chris Tabraham and Doreen Grove
Edinburgh Castle
Iain MacIvor
Stirling Castle
Richard Fawcett
Roman Scotland
David Breeze

Forthcoming:

Celtic Scotland
Ian Armit
Industrial Scotland
John Hume
Scottish Castles
Chris Tabraham
Scottish Cathedrals
Richard Fawcett
Scottish Palaces
Denys Pringle
Iona
Anna Ritchie
St Andrews
Richard Fawcett